Menstruating women dancing.

Ancient rock art painting from the Pilbara region, in northwestern Australia.

ALSO BY ANITA DIAMANT

Fiction

The Boston Girl
Day After Night
The Last Days of Dogtown
Good Harbor
The Red Tent

Nonfiction

*Pitching My Tent: On Marriage, Motherhood, and Other
Leaps of Faith*

The Jewish Wedding Now

The New Jewish Baby Book: Names, Ceremonies, and Customs

*Bible Baby Names: Spiritual Choices from
Judeo-Christian Tradition*

Living a Jewish Life: Jewish Traditions, Customs, and Values

How to Raise a Jewish Child

*Choosing a Jewish Life: A Handbook for People
Converting to Judaism*

*Saying Kaddish: How to Comfort the Dying, Bury the Dead, and
Mourn as a Jew*

PERIOD.
END OF SENTENCE.

A New Chapter in the Fight
for Menstrual Justice

Anita Diamant

Foreword by Melissa Berton,
founder of The Pad Project

SCRIBNER

New York   London   Toronto   Sydney   New Delhi

Scribner
An Imprint of Simon & Schuster, Inc.
1230 Avenue of the Americas
New York, NY 10020

First Scribner trade paperback edition May 2021

SCRIBNER and design are registered trademarks of The Gale Group, Inc., used under license by Simon & Schuster, Inc., the publisher of this work.

For information about special discounts for bulk purchases, please contact Simon & Schuster Special Sales at 1-866-506-1949 or business@simonandschuster.com.

The Simon & Schuster Speakers Bureau can bring authors to your live event. For more information or to book an event, contact the Simon & Schuster Speakers Bureau at 1-866-248-3049 or visit our website at www.simonspeakers.com.

Interior design by Wendy Blum

Manufactured in the United States of America

1   3   5   7   9   10   8   6   4   2

Library of Congress Cataloging-in-Publication Data has been applied for.

ISBN 978-1-9821-4428-9
ISBN 978-1-9821-4429-6 (pbk)
ISBN 978-1-9821-4430-2 (ebook)

For the spectacular young people
who are making the change

poem in praise of menstruation

if there is a river
more beautiful than this
bright as the blood
red edge of the moon   if

there is a river
more faithful than this
returning each month
to the same delta   if there

is a river
braver than this
coming and coming in a surge
of passion, of pain   if there is

a river
more ancient than this
daughter of eve
mother of cain and of abel   if there is in

the universe such a river   if
there is some where water
more powerful than this wild
water
pray that it flows also
through animals
beautiful and faithful and ancient
and female and brave

—Lucille Clifton

Contents

Contents

PART FIVE

Foreword

What can we make of messes—of menses? When my daughter, Helen, late to develop as I had been, got her first real period at sixteen, she was cramming for a midterm in the middle seat of the middle row of a large airliner, where she was traveling with me and four of my high school students to New York City to attend the Annual Commission on the Status of Women at the United Nations. She was starting to unbuckle herself when the seat belt sign turned red. I was struggling with my own inner turbulence. What qualified me to be the faculty advisor for this student delegation to the UN? I held no degree in political science or gender studies. I was—and still am—an English teacher. I traffic (or so I scolded myself) in poetry, not policy! Finally, the seat belt light flashed off. By the time of Helen's third trip to the restroom, her friends, seated in the rows behind us, nodded knowingly and handed her tampons, pads, and a packet of Midol as she made her way down the aisle. A change of clothes was in her carry-on. Periods are messy—and so, the saying goes, is life.

The next wintry morning, in an overheated, overcrowded conference room, my students and I first learned about "period poverty," a phrase that would not come into vogue until years later. Period poverty is the lack of access to menstrual products, to clean and safe toilets, to handwashing facilities and waste disposal, and to education about reproductive biology. As a consequence of period poverty, girls around the world, in high-income as well as in low-income countries, miss school when they are menstruating. Some quit school entirely. Surely it is the presence of patriarchy, not the absence of products, that prioritizes the father's house (then the husband's house) above the schoolhouse, but the practical need for pads was something my students and I could understand and act upon.

That afternoon, at a sparsely populated parallel event, we heard about Arunachalam Muruganantham, the Indian inventor whose manual "pad machine" would not only manufacture low-cost, hygienic pads from locally sourced materials but could also spur a microenterprise for the women engaged in the pads' production and distribution. And nearing midnight that same day, in a hotel room littered with empty pizza boxes, half-emptied suitcases, and scattered toiletries, my students and I determined that we would fund-raise to send one of Muruganantham's machines to our partner community in northern India, and that we would document the process on film. At the time that we embarked on what would become a six-year journey to create The Pad Project nonprofit organization and to complete the film *Period. End of Sentence.*, we had no preparation, no plan, no path. What we did have was a group of committed young women who believed with all their hearts that periods should not shut doors to dreams but open them to adulthood in all its opportunities.

Our gumption, we must acknowledge, grew in large measure because we passed through doorways that, for us, privilege had already opened. Our initial team of five was white, from multi-generational college families, and not one of us had ever struggled to buy a box of pads. And yet we met red lights. Turns out, centuries' old stigma doesn't shed as readily as uterine lining. We learned anew that periods were not a polite topic for conversation—much less a documentary. We dug in and gathered strength from the pioneering women's health and human rights activists who came before us, and who make us better every day. The Pad Project's own seedlings took root in relationships with the Oakwood School, Girls Learn International, and Action India: three collaborators without whose foundational soil, water, and sunlight our efforts might never have borne fruit.

The Oakwood School prepared the soil. Founded in 1951, Oakwood, an independent, coeducational K–12 school in North Hollywood, pledges as part of its Statement of Philosophy "to cultivate depth of character; and to instill a lifelong commitment to social justice." Still, having taught at other schools whose motivational talk didn't always match their walk, I did not take it for granted that, when the students and I presented a plan that would require the school to go public about periods, we would be taken seriously. But the headmaster, administrators, and fellow teachers (a majority of whom were men) all pitched in to help. Our student group grew larger, bake sales blossomed into Kickstarter campaigns, and high schoolers led the way as parents, inspired by their daughters' passion, lent their skills to the cause. Family members became mentors, movie producers, legal advisors, accountants, and (when team tensions ran high) social workers. Together, we flew by the seat of our collective pants to secure our maverick director (herself only a few years older than the students); our magnificent Indian production team, Sikhya Entertainment; and the mound of paperwork required to earn The Pad Project's designation as an official 501(c)3 nonprofit.

Girls Learn International provided the water. Founded in 2003, Girls Learn International (GLI), a program of the Feminist Majority

Foundation, conducts its work "on the principle that humanitarianism has no minimum age requirement and that global youth, in particular girls, have a crucial role to play in leading the movement for universal education." GLI not only facilitated Oakwood's student delegation to the United Nations but also introduced us to Action India, GLI's first international chapter. I remember bursting into the Feminist Majority Foundation's office in Los Angeles and excitedly explaining the idea for the documentary when their executive director stopped me. She reached into her drawer to hand me a sample pad from Muruganantham's machine, and then behind her desk to pull a copy of Anita Diamant's *The Red Tent* from her bookshelf and stated flatly: "The world needs to speak up about periods."

Action India supplied the sunlight. Founded in 1976, Action India, a nongovernmental organization based in New Delhi, champions the "participation of women as citizens to claim their entitlements to public health and civic services." The Pad Project and Action India worked together for two years to ensure that the residents of Kathikera would receive the pad machine in good condition, that the raw pad material would be kept dry and safe from summer monsoons, and that the villagers would be prepared for the arrival of our filmmakers. The workers who would make the pads would market them as "Fly" pads because they wanted women to "soar." The next flight I took with Helen and my high school students was to India to screen the first cut of the film for the women of Kathikera. Mothers, daughters, and sisters all crowded on the floor of the largest home in the village, where the film was projected onto a bedsheet affixed to the wall. Although they did not speak English—and we did not speak Hindi—we giggled and grew closer as we watched the film together.

The Pad Project was the fruit. Grounded in the conviction that "a period should end a sentence, not a girl's education," our own mission is "to create and cultivate local and global partnerships to end period stigma and to empower menstruators worldwide." While we know that no number of pads or pad machines can address the complex causes and manifestations of menstrual stigma, we are thrilled that our twenty-six-minute documentary seized forty-five seconds of worldwide attention on the Oscar stage, spoke to so many viewers, and amplified the conversation about menstruation. Since the Netflix release and Academy Award for *Period. End of Sentence.*, The Pad Project has received thousands of messages of encouragement, and hundreds of requests for pad machines and menstrual hygiene products from all over the world. To help meet that demand, The Pad Project joined forces with others, such as the period care brand This Is L., to carry out their 1:1 solidarity model where for every purchase of This Is L., one period care product is made accessible to a person who needs it.

We are proud of The Pad Project's partnerships in Afghanistan, Ghana, Guatemala, India, Kenya, Nepal, Sierra Leone, Sri Lanka, Uganda, and Zanzibar to implement pad machine and washable cloth pad programs, and to support community-led reproductive health and education workshops. Domestically, The Pad Project provides microgrants to grassroots organizations to distribute products in Arizona, California, Louisiana, Maryland, Minnesota, New York, and Rhode Island. In our hometown of Los Angeles, the teenage founders of The Pad Project—now young women in their early twenties—have become part of our small but stellar staff and work with my enthusiastic new students to manage our marketing, communications, events, and newly launched Ambassador Program. Ambassadors for The Pad Project link arms with us to lead the charge for menstrual equity by raising funding and awareness. This year's inaugural class is composed of ninety-five ambassadors from around the world, of all ages, backgrounds, and genders.

Reader, please join us. You need no degree or special expertise. Sometimes the uncharted path leads to the largest clearing, and every student is a teacher. My students show me what I do not know, and although I may not have it right, I suspect I am just now learning the meaning of a poem that I have taught for decades. It is a poem about the power of imperfection. In "The Munich Mannequins," Sylvia Plath recounts her impressions of seeing naked mannequins on display in a storefront window. My students, confronted daily with false ideals of flawless womanhood, can relate to her experience. They feel the force of the poem's first line: "Perfection is terrible, it cannot have children." For my part, I like to imagine the poet, a young mother at thirty as I once was, at that moment when she looks through the window at the mannequins and realizes—maybe even rejoices—that their "perfection is terrible." They cannot change, cannot choose, cannot create. My students will make their own way. Their bodies—whether or not they are bleeding or bearing children—will not define who they become. Plath's life was short, but her words live on: "The blood flood is the flood of love." Let's revel in that miracle. Let's revel in that mess.

Melissa Berton

A Word, First

Menstruator: I use the word "menstruator" in this book to be inclusive of everyone who menstruates, *including* girls, women, nonbinary, and trans people. "Menstruator" and "people who menstruate" widen the circle; they do not erase or cancel women and girls.

Women and girls: I use "women and girls" because menstruation is a gendered experience. Menstrual shame and stigma are expressions of misogyny, the historic distrust and dislike of women in general and the female body in particular. In binary civilizations (which is to say, most), culture, language, religion, and art reflect and reinforce the equation that menstruation = female = less than—a prejudice that extends to trans and nonbinary people.

They: I use a singular "they" and gender-neutral language whenever it better suits, or serves, or just fits nicely into the shape of a sentence. A writer's prerogative.

I'm sure this multiple-choice scheme will annoy some readers and enrage others. It is an attempt to communicate the diversity of menstrual experiences and invite us to get beyond either-or thinking. My hope is that it will create a little breathing room in the new menstrual order that is aborning.

PERIOD.
END OF SENTENCE.

PERIOD
END OF SENTENCE

Introduction

"**I** *wish I had a red tent.*"
Women have been saying that to me ever since *The Red Tent* was published in 1997. I've heard it from women of all ages, races, religious traditions, and from all over the world.

In my novel, menstruation and childbirth took place in a women-only space that acknowledged the body's rhythms and need to rest and recharge; it was where women gave birth in the company of midwives, mothers, sisters, aunts, and friends; where girls learned about the workings of their bodies from the women around them as naturally as they learned their mother tongue.

Dinah, the narrator of *The Red Tent*, describes the menstrual tent as a sanctuary where her mother and mother-aunties "ran their fingers through my curls, repeating the escapades of their youths, the sagas of their childbirths." They "traded secrets like bracelets, and these were handed down to me."

The idea of sharing the experience of menstruating, of time and space to acknowledge and honor the seasons of the female body—communally, safely, intergenerationally, and without shame—struck a chord.

So I wasn't surprised when Melissa Berton, founder of The

Pad Project, asked if I would be interested in writing a book about menstruation. But my enthusiasm for this project had virtually nothing to do with *The Red Tent*; at least I didn't think so at the time. I had been reading stories about menstruation in the news, some from as far away as Nepal and as near as the local high school, all of them revelatory in one way or another. And by the time we talked, I had seen the film.

I was on the couch the night of the 2019 Academy Awards broadcast when the Oscar for short documentary went to *Period. End of Sentence.* In accepting the award, director Rayka Zehtabchi said, "I'm not crying because I'm on my period. I can't believe a movie about menstruation just won an Oscar." Melissa Berton followed her, held the Oscar high, and made a declaration that launched a tweet seen round the world—"A period should end a sentence, not a girl's education."

The audience roared. I jumped off my couch and cheered, certain that a million other people were doing the same. How often do you feel the Earth's axis shift, just a little, in the direction of justice?

The next day, I watched the movie, which follows a group of women in a small rural town on the outskirts of Delhi as they learn to use a simple machine that makes low-cost sanitary pads both for their own use and to create a microbusiness, selling them to neighbors. In telling that story, the film also exposes the profound silence and misinformation that surrounds menstruation and shows how talking and teaching about periods can change lives.

The Oscar broadcast was seen by 26.9 million viewers in 225 countries and territories, creating a huge audience for the film, which is still available on Netflix and the Netflix YouTube channel. The response was overwhelming. In the days and weeks that followed, The Pad Project received thousands of messages from around the world.

Some inquired about getting a pad-making machine for their village, some offered to volunteer or donate money, others wanted to know if they could show the film at their school and to church groups to raise awareness and funds.

The movie also revealed a pent-up need to share personal stories.

Pat in California wrote: I almost cried when I watched the little girls who had never seen or used a pad. I grew up in Compton, and sometimes, as a thirteen-year-old, my family had no money for pads, so I made pads out of old socks.

Isata in Sierra Leone wrote: When my male siblings noticed that I was having my period, they wouldn't eat with me or bathe from the same bucket. It was like I was infected with the Ebola virus and any interaction with me would make them sick.

Elaine in Seattle, Washington, wrote: My thirteen-year-old daughter and I watched your amazing documentary and are inspired. We anticipate that she will start menstruating any day now. To celebrate this developmental milestone, we hope to raise enough funds to purchase one machine.

The film *Period. End of Sentence.* started out as a high school club project at the Oakwood School in North Hollywood. Melissa Berton, an English teacher and advisor to the school's chapter of Girls Learn International, had taken a group of student-delegates to a meeting of the United Nations Commission on the Status of Women. There, they learned about the impact of silence and misinformation about menstruation and were introduced to the story of Arunachalam Muruganantham, an Indian man who invented a simple machine to manufacture low-cost menstrual pads. Outraged by what they learned about menstrual injustice and gender inequality, and inspired by Muruganantham's efforts, the students decided to raise money to donate a machine to the women of a village in India. And because the Oakwood School happens to be in Hollywood, it wasn't a big stretch for them to think about making a documentary to shine a light on efforts to end period poverty.

Fun fact: nobody bet on this movie to win the Oscar. The scuttlebutt in Hollywood was that Academy members—mostly white men of a certain age—would never vote for a movie about menstruation. That it did win follows the arc of the story told in this book, a narrative that begins in shame and silence and ends with Zehtabchi's and Berton's explicit exuberance at the Oscars.

I started my research by signing up on Google alerts for "menstruation" and was immediately overwhelmed by stories about period poverty; efforts to end taxes on pads and tampons; the indignities suffered by poor, homeless, incarcerated, and refugee menstruators; the voices of nonbinary and trans people who menstruate; the movement among student activists demanding free pads and tampons in campus bathrooms, and more. There were heartbreaking stories of lives lost because of period shaming and heartwarming stories of twelve-year-old activists who refuse to be ashamed. It felt like I was trying to fill a teacup from a firehose.

But whatever the angle and whether the story originated in Toronto, Cape Town, London, or Columbus, Ohio, most began by acknowledging the powerful taboo against talking about menstruation and then declared that things were getting better. For example: "The long silence has been broken. Menstruation has ceased to be a subject for whispered confidence." That declaration comes from *The Curse: A Cultural History of Menstruation* by Janice Delaney, Mary Jane Lupton, and Emily Toth, published in 1976.

It is sad and infuriating that, even forty-five-plus years later, we are still announcing a new age of openness, which is not to say that things haven't changed since 1976. In fact, the effort to end menstrual silence, stigma, and injustice, which was more observation than action plan back then, is now a global, diverse, intergenerational, and intersectional movement. It is being written into law and litigated in the courts. Teenagers are going to high school wearing T-shirts that say "Anything you can do, I can do bleeding." Millions of women in India created a 385-mile Wall of Protest to object to a religious ban that kept women of menstruating age from entering a Hindu temple. Even during the COVID-19 pandemic, scores of organizations raised consciousness and money to ensure a supply of period products to those who lacked access to them.

This reckoning is not dissimilar from the #MeToo movement, when sexual harassment and assault burst into plain view after years of quietly "putting up with it." The unwritten rules about putting up with menstrual stigma and shame are ancient, explicitly embedded in religion, culture, and language. After all, periods have been called "the curse" for millennia. (And putting "the curse" in scare quotes does not neutralize the sting.)

Radical change is the order of the day: radical in the sense of uprooting beliefs and habits that treat menstruation as pollution, incapacity, inferiority, and a pre-ordained shame. Radical, too, in the effort to replace those lies (let's be honest) with the understanding that menstruation is a vital sign, an essential part of human design, which is—depending on your belief system—a wonder of nature or a sacred vessel or both.

The goal is nothing less than recognition of the full humanity of women and girls and everyone who menstruates. In other words, the end of sexism and misogyny.

This book is not comprehensive or exhaustive, which would be impossible given the rate of change. It's a kind of album of moments in the ongoing multifaceted movement to end menstrual injustice, including examples of cruelty, oppression, and outrage, but also of inspiration, humor, beauty, solidarity, and hope. I have made every effort to be accurate, but like all albums this one is personal rather than definitive.

I think the story of menstruation is at an inflection point—the place in a curve where you can sense a change of course. We're still carrying a lot of heavy baggage and we've got a long way to go, but we've got momentum and more than enough good news to keep us moving forward.

And the best news is the way many young people are simply unwilling to put up with the bad old rules, like the sixteen-year-old who stormed home after school and demanded, "Why should I have to hide my pads?"

Her mother answered, "Because nobody ever asked the question before."

"Well," said the girl, "I'm not going to do it."

Period! End of sentence!

PART ONE

The Curse

Hansa, Northern Ethiopia: "In my community, they refer to women during menstruation as 'cursed.' No one talks about it. During my period, I refrain from normal activities like going to work or to the market because I feel ashamed and I want to hide myself."

What's in a name? At any given moment, there are 800 million people menstruating on Planet Earth—and as many as five thousand euphemisms for menstruation in use: folksy (Aunt Flo), descriptive (on the rag), sweet (Germany's strawberry week), alarming (Finland's mad cow disease), historical (from France, the English have landed), familial (Little sister, in China), and anecdotal (South Africa's, Granny's stuck in traffic).

"Period" is the most common euphemism, used around the world and by people who speak Amharic, German, Russian, Spanish, and Xhosa, among others. And even though "period" refers only to an interval of time and doesn't hint at blood or bodies, people still drop their voices when the word comes up in conversation.

Then there is "the curse."

Menstruation has been defined and described as a curse from ancient times to the present: stamped as truth by scholars, enforced by religious leaders, and passed down—a miserable legacy—through generations of women. As a result, for millions of people, "cursed" is an accurate description of how it feels to live in a body that bleeds.

A curse is a magical formula or potion that does harm: the death of the firstborn, princes into frogs, red hair. An illness or generational misfortune is sometimes called a curse.

The curse is one and only one bloody thing. It identifies a necessary part of human reproduction as a malediction, and by extension, anyone who menstruates as a threat.

From early on, Western civilization considered menstruation a threat. In first-century Rome, the scholar Pliny the Elder wrote that contact with menstrual blood "turns new wine sour, crops touched by it become barren, grafts die, seeds in gardens are dried up, the fruit of trees fall off, the edge of steel and the gleam of ivory are dulled, hives of bees die, even bronze and iron are at once seized by rust, and a horrible smell fills the air; to taste it drives dogs mad and infects their bites with an incurable poison."

If that sounds laughably outdated, in the 1920s, *The Lancet*, an esteemed medical journal, reported that the touch of menstruating women caused cut flowers to wilt, and in 1974 doubled down with an article asserting that a permanent wave would not "take" in the hair of menstruating women.

The world's major religions have treated menstruation as a pollutant, a punishment, or, at the least, a problem. Jewish law and practice are based on passages from Leviticus, including this one: "When a woman has a discharge, her discharge being blood from her body, she shall remain in her impurity seven days; whoever touches her shall be unclean until evening. Anything that she lies on during her impurity shall be unclean, and anything that she sits on shall be unclean." In the Middle Ages, Nachmanides, a leading rabbi, scholar, and physician, maintained that "if a menstruating woman stares at a mirror of polished iron, drops of blood will appear on it."

In Jewish practice, the problem of impurity was solved by mandating set times and terms of separation in the rubric of "family purity" (*taharat hamishpacha*). After menstruation, women are to immerse in water, specifically in a ritual bath called a *mikveh* before they can be sexually available to their husbands. Observance of the menstrual laws has varied among Jewish communities and changed over time; it continues among Orthodox/observant women and has been reinterpreted and adopted by some liberal/feminist Jews (see page 50–51).

"The curse of Eve" is a common Christian characterization of the punishment meted out to the first woman and all subsequent women: "Unto the woman He said, I will greatly multiply thy sorrow and thy conception; in sorrow thou shalt bring forth children." Blood is part of the "sorrow" of bringing forth children. The Catholic Church's rule against the ordination of women was, to some extent, based on their "ritual uncleanness." Most Christian denominations do not follow specific rituals or laws regarding menstruation, though most reflect the local culture's attitudes. Some Orthodox Christian traditions discourage or even forbid menstruating women from attending church or receiving communion.

For Hindus, menstrual restrictions are based on a sin committed by Lord Indra (King of the Gods) for killing a Brahmin named Vishwaroopacharya. To rid himself of guilt for the murder, Indra divided his sin into three parts and distributed one third to the land, one third to the trees, and one third to women, who from then on began to menstruate and bear children. Indra's sin is the reason that menstruating women are denied entry to some Hindu holy sites, and why women are barred from handling food for or sleeping under the same roof as their families. Mohandas Gandhi, who was a spiritual as well as political leader, said menstruation was a "distortion of women's soul because of their sexuality."

> *In 2011, Pravin Nikam was a young engineering student visiting Assam when he met a young girl. "She was weaving a sari on a hand loom," he said. "I asked what school did she go to? She said, 'I don't go to school. I am cursed by God.'*
>
> *"I asked the same question of her father, who said, 'In our community, when girls start to menstruate, we do not send them to the school because they are cursed.'"*

Like Judaism, Islam considers menstruating women unclean and prohibits husbands from touching their wives during their periods; it also excuses—or restricts—menstruating women from reciting the five daily prayers, entering mosques, touching the Quran, and fasting during Ramadan. While the Prophet Muhammad classified menstruation as originating from Satan, the Quran lists it with other ordinary bodily functions such as yawning in prayer and sneezing.

According to Buddhist teaching, menstruation is nothing more than a "natural physical exertion," but local practices and contact with Hindu culture subsumed that belief. Japanese Buddhists prohibit menstruating women from approaching some sacred sites, and among Tibetan Buddhists, menstruating women are considered a danger to themselves and others because of the belief that ghosts feed on blood.

Period. End of Sentence.

Periods can be uncomfortable, inconvenient, embarrassing, and all kinds of painful, from mild cramps to ones that keep you in bed for days. Periods are expensive, messy, and unpredictable. Comedian Michelle Wolf, the doyenne of period jokes, compares menstruation to an outdoor cat. "You know it's coming back. You just don't know when."

Menstruation is also a mark of maturity and a measure of health. Metaphorically and spiritually, it signals the continuity of human life.

Stigma and powerlessness can make it feel like punishment. But menstruation is not the curse.

The curse is shame.

Shame

Lupita Nyong'o was in the audience the night that *Period. End of Sentence.* won an Academy Award for best short documentary. The actress stood up and applauded when the prize was announced. After she watched the film, she realized, "I was not free of the shame that comes with bleeding every month, and how much ignorance there is about what a period is."

"Shaming the cycle of a woman leads to a cycle of shame," said Nyong'o. "When a woman is not permitted to accept her body, how can we expect her to stand up for her body when it's being abused?"

Menstrual shame keeps women from seeking medical help for pain. It's why girls who can't afford pads or tampons stay home from school rather than risk bleeding through their clothes— something that happens in Germany as well as Sierra Leone. It's what keeps teachers from teaching their students about periods.

Nobody is born with an innate sense of shame about menstruation: it must be taught. And the message doesn't have to be as explicit as "you are cursed." Unspoken scorn, institutional exclusion, and the example of the women around you sends the message, loud and clear.

The harm is not equally distributed. And while privilege and education can mitigate the harm, virtually everybody who menstruates knows how it feels to be ashamed of your body, ashamed of yourself.

According to a 2018 survey of attitudes toward menstruation in New Zealand and Australia, more than half of thirteen-to-seventeen-year-old girls interviewed said they would rather fail a school test than have their classmates know they're on their period.

Amanda in South Africa wrote: "One fateful day at school, I was writing my math exam. I remember I was on question 6 when I started to feel wet on my skirt. I had to stand up to get another sheet of paper to finish my exam, but with bloodstains on my skirt, I couldn't. At the end of the test, my teacher asked why I didn't hand it to him. He was a man so I couldn't tell him. I just kept quiet and gave what I had finished to him when he was near me.

"I cried and ran out without anybody's permission. I went home and stayed in my room. After three days I gathered some courage and went back, but I found I was behind with my schoolwork. Not finishing the exam resulted in me not getting my full marks. This day always comes back to my mind and it really hurts. . . . Being on periods can make someone get left behind on many things, trust me."

In some cultures, menstruating women are banished and survive in misery. In Nepal, menstrual sequestration is called *chhaupadi*—a word that means impure—and it is dangerous. In this ancient Hindu custom, which is practiced in a few rural parts of the country, menstruating women are barred from sleeping under the same roof as their families because of the belief that their presence will sicken others. Women, who often take their young children with them, spend nights in crude shelters: huts, lean-tos, caves, even stables.

In January 2019, Partabi Bogati died of smoke inhalation while trying to keep warm in the tiny shed where she slept during her period. A month earlier, Amba Bohara and her two young children also died of suffocation. Six months before that, it was Gauri Kumari Bayak, who had been leading birth control classes and telling women to stand up for themselves; even she could not bring herself to resist community norms.

In the small town of Sitatoli in central India, women on their periods are sent to an eight-foot-square windowless mud hut known as a *kurma ghar*. A place without electricity or running water, where women sleep on the floor and get drenched when it rains. Between 2011 and 2018, at least eight women died in the *kurma ghar* of another town in the Gadchiroli district, mostly from pneumonia or snake bites.

Anyone who refused to go to the *kurma ghar* was called up in front of the village and ordered to buy liquor and cook a meal of chicken for the whole community—a steep price. One woman said, "It's better to obey."

Menstrual Shame

Menstrual shame is a brew of *silence, lack of knowledge*, and *stigma*. Each poses a threat to health and happiness; in combination they can be toxic, even deadly.

Silence

Silence starts at home. A little boy finds a box of his mother's pads hidden under a bed. He asks her what they're for: she slaps him and warns him to never talk about such things again. Period. End of conversation.

A girl tells her mother that she's bleeding for the first time and she is told, "You're a woman now. Don't tell your father. Don't tell anyone." Period. End of conversation.

"Don't tell" becomes a reflex. Comedian Michelle Wolf imagines the scene over a backyard fence where a woman—worried about a symptom—begins to ask her neighbor, "Have you ever..."

She stops mid-sentence and says, "No. Never mind. I'd rather die than have this conversation."

Silence about menstruation casts a cloak of invisibility—and worse, of unknowing—over the evidence of our senses. A man who grew up in a middle-class home in Mumbai barely noticed that his mother stayed out of the kitchen for a few days every month, and somehow he knew not to ask about it. "It wasn't until years later that I understood."

Some parents assume that their children will learn about menstruation in school, if not in science class then certainly in a health or sex education session, but that isn't likely. Information about menstruation is often passed over. In a 2019 poll of a thousand American teens, 76 percent said they were taught more about the biology of frogs than about the biology of the female human body. In a similar study from Quetta, Pakistan, 78 percent of girls polled reported that there was no mention of menstruation in school.

In spite of the pressure to say nothing, word gets out. Someone gets a book, someone's brother finds a site on the internet, an older sister shares what she heard from her friends . . . and the grapevine curriculum is full of whoppers:

- If you bathe during your period, you won't be able to have a baby.

- If you touch milk it will curdle.

- If a man sees your menstrual blood, he will go blind.

- You have to change your pad every hour or you'll get sick.

- If anyone sees your menstrual blood, you will become infertile.

There are some instances where silence is a protective strategy, as when first menstruation means a girl is marriageable and families try to hide their twelve-year-old's first period, so she won't be sought—or stolen—as a bride.

But in general, secrecy is a threat to health, well-being, and a barrier to basic menstrual literacy.

Lack of Knowledge

According to a 2019 UNICEF study, 50 percent of girls in Afghanistan knew nothing about menstruation until they had their first period. Nearly the same results came out of a survey in the UK, where 47 percent of women polled said they were completely unprepared.

Ignorance is the opposite of bliss, and in the absence of facts, fear and misinformation flourish:

- I thought I had hurt myself.

- I thought I had cancer.

- I thought I was dying.

Chris Bobel, associate professor of Women's, Gender, and Sexuality Studies at the University of Massachusetts, Boston, describes this as the menstrual mandate: "Keep your menstrual status to yourself. Hide menstrual care products. Deny your body, buck up, and move on! This is 'a gag order,'" says Bobel, and it does untold damage.

Dr. Jen Gunter, author of *The Vagina Bible*, calls this "medical gaslighting." Gunter recalls going to the gynecologist as a young woman and asking about her periods, which were "catastrophically heavy." The doctor said that her symptoms were normal, though she later found out that her heavy flow had led to an iron deficiency.

"I want to blame the doctor for dismissing me, but I have complex feelings," she writes. "She had probably trained in the 1960s. What would she have been taught about menstruation? Probably very little, beyond the fact that it existed." For a long time, medicine viewed "female complaints" as examples of weakness or "hysteria." To this day, the normalizing of menstrual pain by doctors combined with lack of information about menstruation can lead to missed diagnoses of endometriosis, fibroid tumors, and polycystic ovary syndrome (PCOS), which affects one in ten American women. Heavy bleeding can also be a symptom of cervical and uterine cancers, which may be fatal if untreated.

Basic menstrual literacy is essential and potentially life-saving. Everyone needs to know that a "normal" period is different for everybody and that it can vary in individuals from month to month, year to year, regular/irregular, light/heavy, spotting/no spotting.

And everyone—especially providers—has to be alert to symptoms that call for medical evaluation: having to change a pad or tampon hourly, pain so bad you can't get out of bed for a day or two, periods that keep you from normal activities or last longer than a week. As much as this sounds like common sense, it was only in 2015 that the American College of Obstetricians and Gynecologists began recommending doctors consider menstrual history as a vital sign—and not a moment too soon. In 2020, the *British Medical Journal* published a report based on a twenty-four-year study showing that women's periods could act as a barometer for general health, with irregular menstruation and longer cycles associated with greater risk of dying before the age of seventy.

Stigma

Stigma is the public face of menstrual shame. According to the *Cambridge Dictionary*, stigma is: "A strong feeling of disapproval that most people in a society have about something, especially when this is unfair."

Menstrual stigma can become a real threat to health: cloth pads—which are effective, inexpensive, and environmentally friendly—must be washed and thoroughly dried. Drying them in the sun is an effective disinfectant, but if menstruation has to be kept secret at all costs, women who live in rainy climates may have to use damp pads, which can harbor harmful bacteria.

Stigma can be as subtle as the way a cashier picks up your box of tampons with two fingers and drops it into a bag in the blink of an eye.

Stigma can be as blatant as a sign on a Hindu temple that reads: "Attention: Women are not allowed to enter the temple during menstruation."

But mostly, stigma is so commonplace, it barely registers. The language used to describe and sell menstrual products suggests a covert war against a shrewd opponent. The word "fresh" on a box of pads implies a battle against "foul." "Sanitary" counters the threat of "soiled." "Carefree" responds to "distress," and "hygiene" holds the line against "disease." In India, Procter & Gamble markets a pad called Whisper.

The aisles where freshness is sold usually feature signage for "Feminine Hygiene" or "Feminine Care." "Feminine" sends a very specific message: *"Having qualities or an appearance traditionally associated with women, especially delicacy and prettiness."*

Putting "feminine" above the shelf where tampons are sold is a signal that boys and men need not enter because . . . *ewwww.* "Feminine" erases the presence of trans and nonbinary menstruators, butch lesbians, as well as women who reject the word as archaic and ill-fitting as a corset. The signs might as well say "Unmentionable Products for Ladies Only."

Stigma is passed from generation to generation, teacher to student, and from parent to child. If parents are uncomfortable with the subject—if they banish it altogether or speak of it with thinly veiled disgust—children get the message that periods are repulsive and assume that people who have periods are repulsive, too.

But children are inoculated against the worst effects of stigma and shame if parents are comfortable talking about periods. If they say all the words (menstruation, vagina, cramps, tampons) and if they are unhurried and open-ended, as in "Ask me anything about periods whenever you want to. And if I don't know the answer, we'll look it up together."

Period Shaming

Because menstrual stigma tends to fly under the radar, it takes genuine outrage to attract international headlines, which is what happened when a Hindu priest in Gujarat, India, proclaimed that women who cook during their periods would be reborn as dogs. The ensuing protests included a Period Feast in Delhi, with music, balloons, and food cooked in public by women wearing aprons that said "I am a proud menstruating woman." No sooner had that story faded from the news when reports surfaced about staff members at a college associated with the same guru forcing some sixty students to remove their underwear to see if they were bleeding.

Most period shaming is far less dramatic. Someone makes a wisecrack about your request for a tampon or asks if you're going to the bathroom again because you're on the rag. Even when meant as jokes, comments like that can land like a threat.

Women and girls are taught to ignore all such "teasing," because that only draws more attention to your secret, which is to say, your shame. Fear of exposure can be a source of anxiety, worry, preoccupation, or mortification—from *mors*, the Latin word for death.

On August 31, 2017, BBC News ran an item under the headline, "India girl kills herself over 'menstruation shaming.'" The story—about a twelve-year-old schoolgirl who killed herself after a teacher allegedly humiliated her over a menstrual bloodstain—was picked up by media around the world. Educators, government officials,

23

health and women's rights advocates expressed outrage and called for improved education, better access to period products, and an end to the legacy of shame. As time passed, the twelve-year-old became a symbol of menstrual injustice, her life virtually erased by her death.

BBC News, August 31, 2017, India girl kills herself over "menstruation shaming." "A twelve-year-old schoolgirl from southern India has killed herself after a teacher allegedly humiliated her over a bloodstain from menstruation."

Safreena* lived in Southern India, in a relatively small city of modest houses painted in bright shades of blue and pink. She shared a typical two-room dwelling with her parents and younger brother and attended a co-ed school that styled itself a "progressive English school." She was an average student, which did not satisfy her father who sometimes beat her for not meeting his expectations.

Safreena was described as calm and quietly confident, yet she was afraid of the neighborhood goats and chickens and scared of the dark; if she woke in the night needing to go to the toilet outside, she'd wake her mother to go with her.

Safreena wanted to be a teacher when she grew up—though she was also interested in hotel management. She was good at yoga. Her father, an autorickshaw driver, could be abusive when he drank. Her mother says she had stopped him from hitting their daughter with a cane by telling him she had her period.

Safreena knew very little about menstruation. When she got her period, her mother told her only what she had

---

* Pseudonym.

been told: "You're a big girl. Don't tell anyone. Girls of a cer-tain age get a period and don't roam around."

Safreena kept asking why, but her mother didn't answer.

During her first period, she stayed home from school for a week. When Safreena returned, her mother says that she was beaten with a cane and made to kneel on the floor as punishment for missing class and not completing her home-work. After that, she never stayed home for more than a day.

Safreena bled through her school uniform on a Friday. Her father picked her up from school at 5:30, as usual. She didn't tell him what happened, but later that night, she told her mother that her teacher had made her show the stain to everyone in class, then threw the rag she used to wipe the blackboard at her.

On Sunday, the night before she was to return to school, she asked her mother if her uniform was ready. Later that night, she wrote a suicide note and went to the roof.

Safreena's death was covered by Indian media for weeks and reported around the world. The police investigated. Her teacher was discharged. Public health officials voiced outrage. Many students transferred to other schools. None of her friends or neighbors would go on record about what had happened.

The secretary of the local Rotary club dismissed the idea that Safreena's suicide was related to her period. If that had been the case, he said, "It should have happened within two or three hours." He thought the family had been urged to "go public in order to make money from the school, because the teacher shouted at her."

Safreena did not mention her period in her note, which began, "Ma, please forgive me. I don't know what to do but I have to die." She wrote that her teacher was always "com-plaining against me.

"What crime did I commit? Why is she troubling me so much?"

She wrote that her father believed what the teacher told him and thought that she was lying. "I have no option but to commit suicide."

Sometime in the middle of the night on August 27, 2017, twelve-year-old Safreena tiptoed to the roof of the two-story house next door and jumped. It appeared that some electric wires broke her fall, so it is possible that she did not die immediately when she hit the ground.

Her parents found her in the morning.

Safreena's story is uncommon but not unique.

Two years after Safreena died, on September 6, 2019, Jackline Chepngeno, a fourteen-year-old girl in the village of Kabiangek, Kenya, committed suicide after being humiliated by a teacher because of bloodstains on her clothes.

But Jackline's community rose up to protest her death. The next day, two hundred parents rioted at the school, and Jackline's mother told her daughter's story on Kenyan television. Her uncle started a social media campaign to #EndPeriodShame, #EndwithJackline. Within a week, eleven Kenyan women members of parliament "laid siege" (as the Honorable Esther Passaris tweeted) at the Ministry of Education in protest.

There is a terrible irony to the fact that this story originated in Kenya, which has been praised as an international leader in menstrual policy: it was the first country to repeal the value-added tax on period products in 2004, and in 2011, the government budgeted funds to provide them in schools. As of 2017, the government was required to supply pads to "every school-going girl who has reached puberty," but those regulations were never fully funded or implemented, so there were no period supplies at Jackline's school.

The lack of a pad wasn't the cause of Jackline's death—or of Safreena's. Bleeding through your clothes in school is a nightmare, but the thing that turns an accident into a catastrophe is shame.

Shamelessness:
The Changing of the Guard

At 14, I hadn't yet learned the ropes of carrying pads and aspirin in my bag, or mastered tracking my flow. I was new to being a woman. So, when the first ache hit in the middle of religion class, I knew I was screwed. I had no pads, and the sanitary napkin vending machines in the restroom weren't free.

The teacher, Mr. Jones,* was a drill sergeant: Catholic, bald, tall, always shouting. He was strict and had a knack for picking out nervous students for the morning prayer presentation.

"Jesus comes when you need him most," Mr. Jones said, a hand in the air. It was time for student prayer reflections. He closed his Bible and looked right at me. I prayed he would pick someone else.

"Ashlie, you're up!"

I didn't move. I couldn't.

He was standing by my desk. "Ashlie, I said you're up."

"I'm not feeling well," I said. "I'd like to sit this one out."

"Ashlie..."

---

* Pseudonym.

"But I have . . ." I began, but the words "my period" wouldn't tumble out. For a normal phenomenon that has over 5,000 slang terms, it was never talked about in public without hushed tones and uncomfortable faces. Going to an all-girls religious high school was worse. Talking about anything below your waist was blasphemy.

Slowly, I picked up my Bible and made my way to the podium. The moment I got up the whole room came to a quiet halt.

"Holy hell," someone gasped behind me.

I imagined flinging the Bible at Mr. Jones's head and making a run for the door. Instead, I cracked the good book open.

"Ashlie . . ." Mr. Jones's face grew red.

"Psalms 56:11," I read. "In God I have put my trust, I shall not be afraid. What can man do to me?"

On my seat was a red stain the size of my palm. On my desk, a pad from a classmate. "Why don't you just go to the bathroom?" said Mr. Jones.

I did not look at him. I closed the Bible, took the sanitary napkin, and walked out of class and into the nurse's office. She gave me one look, an understanding smile, and two ibuprofens. Then she helped me cover the stain on my jeans with a towel while I took a nap in the spare room.

Four years later, Menstrual Hygiene Day was celebrated for the first time worldwide. It's meant to spark conversation about period stigma, hygiene practices, and the importance of sanitary products for people around the world.

The inability to talk openly about my menses made me ashamed of my body, but Menstrual Hygiene Day gave me the words and confidence to be okay with menstruating.

I talked with my younger cousins who were going to the

same school I did. I told them about discharge and how to put in tampons. I learned that by talking about periods, I normalized it, and that's how I gained confidence. The conversations stopped embarrassing me, and so did my period.

And today, I carry pads and aspirin with me every day of the month, just in case somebody needs a friend.

My Period Made Me an Atheist
by Ashlie Juarbe

On June 28, 2018, Danielle Rowley, a member of parliament, rose to her feet in the United Kingdom's House of Commons and said, "I would like to announce to the House that perhaps you will excuse me for my lateness, that today I am on my period. It's cost me this week already 25 pounds. The average cost of a period in the UK over a year is 500 pounds. Many women cannot afford this."

At any other point in history, a woman who got up in the House of Commons and calmly detailed her menstrual status would have been dragged out by the hair. But MP Rowley's comments were duly reported in the press without a whiff of controversy. Now that women in positions of authority are no longer curiosities, menstruation is on the agenda as never before.

Danielle Rowley is a Millennial (those born between 1981 and 1996), as is Nikita Azad, who started an international protest called #happytobleed after an Indian cleric tried to banish all women from his shrine to prevent any chance of menstrual "pollution." Hundreds of young women posted images of themselves on Twitter holding #happytobleed" signs; also "We Bleed. Get Over It." and "That red spot on my white skirt is NOT obscene."

In response to objections over the use of "happy," Azad raised a virtual eyebrow and said, "We are using 'happy' to express sarcasm—

as a satire, to taunt the authorities, the patriarchal forces which attach impurity with menstruation. [Menstruation] may be painful, but it's perfectly normal to bleed and it does not make me impure."

Cheekiness is a theme among young menstrual disrupters. #happyperiod was founded in the mid-2010s, when Chelsea VonChaz (born 1988) saw a homeless woman bleeding through her pants in downtown Los Angeles's Skid Row. She recruited some friends to distribute period products at shelters, and after four months of packing boxes and delivering them to shelters, she decided to create a nonprofit organization. "My mom came up with the name," she says.

"Millennials are definitely way more open to talking about their periods," says VonChaz. "It really depends on how they were raised and if they're white or a person of color . . . Women of color, we talk less about our periods."

Millennials of color are working to change that. Bria Gadsden is the co-founder and executive director of Love Your Menses, a Boston-based nonprofit founded to "connect girls, young women, and menstruators with the resources they need in order to have healthy menstrual cycles." Gadsden knows that the name of her organization is edgy. "I don't love my period when I have bad cramps," she says. "But this is about loving your body, and that's an important message for Black girls who have been viewed as 'less than' and not taught to value our own selves."

Love Your Menses supplies period products where they are needed and sponsors education programs attended by pre-teens, teens, their mothers, and other adults. Sessions cover anatomy, physiology, self-care, and period products, and give girls a chance to share their own period stories. Gadsden says, "The long-term goal is to train peer educators; to uplift the next generation."

Millennials and Gen Z women (born between 1997 and 2012) grew up with powerful female role models, including elite athletes, Supreme Court justices, and artists, and have produced teenage world-class disrupters and truth-tellers like climate change champion Greta Thunberg and gun-control spokesperson Emma González.

These are generations with little patience for, in the words of Emma González, "Bullshit."

In a 2019 survey, two thousand young American women were asked to agree or disagree with a series of statements about periods:

- "Menstruation isn't gross." Yes said 79 percent of Millennials and 84 percent of Gen Z respondents.

- "Menstruation is a women's issue that men shouldn't discuss." Yes from 28 percent of Millennials, but only 17 percent of Gen Z.

- "Menstruation is treated as a natural process in society." Thirty-five percent of Millennials were okay with that optimistic assessment, but only 19 percent of Gen Z concurred—a difference that suggests that younger women are becoming increasingly aware of and impatient with menstrual stigma.

Jane Henry was only fifteen when she started distributing pads to women in Gauteng Province, South Africa, which includes Johannesburg and Pretoria. That experience led to her founding Once-a-Month in 2019, a nonprofit that supplies pads for those who need them and also runs health and wellness seminars.

In the fall of 2019, Twitter lit up over a picture of cookies that looked like tampons: "My friend's 7th grader goes to a school where the kids organized for free tampons in the bathroom. The male principal said no because they would 'abuse the privilege.' The kids decided to stage a cookie protest."

Judges on the *Great British Baking Show* might have quibbled about the lack of consistency in size, but the cookies were anatomically correct, down to the strings and hints of bright red frosting. Their message was loud, clear, and delicious: "You can't make us feel bad about our periods." Also, "We're mad as hell and we're going to have fun taking you down a peg."

Tens of thousands of shared tweets later, the principal relented. The girls dubbed themselves the Revolutionary Girls Baking Society, "baking a difference one bizarre confection at a time."

That same year, Brookline, Massachusetts, high school senior Sarah Groustra wrote an opinion piece about menstrual stigma for her school newspaper, arguing that period supplies should be available in school bathrooms for free because they are a necessity, just as toilet paper is a necessity. Her article inspired a local official to propose putting free pads and tampons in all public restrooms. The measure passed, making Brookline the first municipality in the United States to do the right thing.

When stories about people like Chelsea VonChaz, Jane Henry, and Sarah Groustra appear in local news outlets, the stories can seem like one-offs, as if Chelsea, Jane, or Sarah weren't part of something much bigger. But the girls know it. As the seventh graders of the Revolutionary Girls Baking Society wrote: "Stand with us and work locally, nationally, and internationally to support the health and rights of all people."

Girls who challenge menstrual taboos have proven to be powerful influencers, and the documentary *Period. End of Sentence.* is an especially potent case in point. The movie not only opened people's eyes to the damage done by silence, stigma, and ignorance about menstruation, but the fact that its producers were a group of high school girls inspired countless people—especially young women—to action.

Simone of Concord, North Carolina, wrote: I am a high school senior. I first became acquainted with The Pad Project while watching the Oscars. The following Tuesday I proposed a school fund-raising screening of the documentary in an Amnesty International meeting.

My high school has a number of girls who lack access to sanitary products, a fact that I was not aware of until my teacher told me that almost every female teacher has been asked by students for pads. What's more, while the school nurse does provide products, she has to pay for them out of her own paycheck.

The people who saw your film . . . not only learned about girls' experience in developing countries, but also witnessed a transparent and mature conversation about menstruation. We often shy away from addressing menstruation as the natural thing it is. Your film provided the opportunity to dismantle this stigma, a positive sign that impacts my town and the world.

Beyoncé has asked, "Who run the world?" And Beyoncé has answered, "Girls."

The Revolutionary Girls Baking Society website declared victory. "Our principal and the school board are now working to make sure every girl in our town will have the products they need readily available, so no girl misses a day of school.... Ours is a story of standing up with love and courage for our basic rights.... If tampon cookies can spark a revolution, then the possibilities are endless!"

This shameless, hands-on-hips period-positive attitude is on the rise.

There may be no better—or more outrageous—example of menstrual shamelessness than the period party—especially when the new menstruator is in charge of the guest list (sometimes gender-inclusive) and the menu, heavy on chocolate and chips, hold the salad. When parents do the planning, there's a tendency to buy matching napkins, add a poem about the moon, and a teary "Sunrise/Sunset" speech.

In 2019, comedian Bert Kreischer spent four minutes on *Conan* talking about his daughters' periods. When his younger girl got hers, there was no question but that she'd have a party like her big sister. Since Kreischer's wife wasn't available to do the shopping, he was sent out to buy snacks and a red velvet cake.

The big day happened to fall on Friday the thirteenth, so his daughter decided to decorate her cake with red frosting that spelled out "Jason"—a nod to the murderer in the bloody *Friday the 13th* horror movies.

Gross! Outrageous! Funny! And perfectly shameless.

Period parties are unapologetic about the icky stuff—body parts, stains, cramps—because laughter is an especially potent antidote to the effects of shame. One custom-in-the-making is to ask guests to bring a box of pads or tampons to donate to a local shelter or food pantry. Which makes everyone in the room part of the movement for menstrual justice.

Millennials and Gen Z women are out in front of this struggle as they are in other important efforts for social change, including the Movement for Black Lives, founded by Millennials Patrisse Cullors, Alicia Garza, and Opal Tometi. Generation Z's international disrupters include Greta Thunberg, Emma González, and education advocate Malala Yousafzai, who at seventeen was the youngest person to win a Nobel Peace Prize.

It's no surprise that these are the most shamelessly period-positive generations in history.

PART TWO

R.E.S.P.E.C.T.

Menstruation = curse has never been a universal equation. There have always been cultures where menstruation was a respected fact of life, where a period—the time itself—was honored, and where the occasion of a girl's first menses was cause for celebration.

If that comes as news, it's because women's history is still mostly unknown, lost, or erased. There is an emerging period-positive counter-narrative of songs, stories, recipes, dances, family traditions, and prayers.

For Native women, the process of retrieving and reanimating lost/suppressed menstrual traditions both honors their past and is building a bridge to a healthier future.

Indigenous Wisdoms

When European powers stole/settled the homelands of Indigenous people in North America, Africa, and the South Pacific, their ancestral beliefs and practices were demonized and banned. Settlers, missionaries, and rulers did everything in their power to suppress, outlaw, and erase them. Some governments kidnapped children and placed them in white homes or boarding schools where they were beaten for speaking their mother tongue and prevented from learning anything about their own culture. In some cases, laws were passed forbidding Native people from observing their sacred rites—including the celebration of menarche. Well into the early twentieth century, anthropologists (mostly men), who rarely spoke to the women in the communities they studied, described menstrual practices (if they noticed them at all) as primitive and oppressive.

During centuries of cultural repression, memory became a form of resistance. Traditional beliefs and practices were preserved by grandparents, who recounted stories they'd heard from their grandparents, and these have been passed down to women who were reclaiming their birthright. Scholar-activist Cutcha Risling

Baldy calls this (re)writing, (re)righting, and (re)riting the historical record.

Risling Baldy, associate professor of Native American Studies at Humboldt State University, is a member of the Hoopa Valley Tribe in Northern California. In her book, *We Are Dancing for You: Native Feminism and the Revitalization of Women's Coming-of-Age Ceremonies*, she blends ethnography, memoir, and political analysis to give voice to the women of her community, past and present.

The Flower Dance

One of Risling Baldy's primary sources was her mother, Lois Risling, a tribal elder, trained medicine woman, and educator, who shared a story about her first menstruation:

Risling told her daughter about being in sixth grade when the teacher called her to the front of the classroom and whispered that she should go to the nurse because she was sick.

Risling told him that she was not sick, but he insisted, so she went, thinking she had a horrible disease. The school nurse told her she was menstruating and called her parents to take her home. "Because I was sick."

At home, she told her grandfather, "I'm sick. I started bleeding. I'm sick."

But her grandfather said she was not sick. He told her that she was a woman, and should be glad, and that good things were going to happen to her. He sent her brothers to the store to buy pads for her. They were not happy about that, but their grandfather said they should be proud.

He apologized for not knowing the Flower Dance song—the traditional song for a new menstruator—so he sang her another.

"It was a recognition of the importance of it," Risling said. "And he just kept saying, 'You are not sick. You are not sick.'

"So, I wasn't sick."

The Flower Dance is a centuries-old test of physical, mental, and spiritual strength and endurance. The girl marking the onset of her period—the *kinahldung*—runs long distances along special paths, stopping to rest at sacred pools. She meditates, fasts, and sings. Some of the challenge requires solitude, but at other times, the community sings, drums, and dances with her; the Hoopa name for the Flower Dance is *Ch'ilwa:l*, which means "they beat time with sticks." The ritual culminates with a feast where the girl receives gifts and—because women are considered especially powerful during their first menses—she bestows blessings on others.

The Flower Dance celebration, once central to the Hoopas, had all but disappeared until Lois Risling and other women of her tribe reclaimed it for their daughters and granddaughters. In 2001, Kayla Rae Begay became the first *kinahldung* in memory to celebrate publicly with her tribe.

Begay wore the traditional maple bark skirt and blue jay feather visor as she ran, sang, and received blessings. "That actual experience, living that experience in my body, has given me knowledge on how to be a Hoopa woman," says Begay.

Her Flower Dance launched a revival that changed Hoopa life for many. Risling Baldy says that her own daughter has grown up looking forward to her Flower Dance. "She does not know a time when men and women did not come together to celebrate a girl and her first menstruation."

In a time when the high school dropout rate among Native

Americans is greater than any group in the country, and Native women and girls experience terrible rates of substance abuse, violence, and rape, the revival of *Ch'ilwa:l* is a source of self-esteem and resilience. It is, says Risling Baldy, "a tangible, physical, spiritual, and communal act of healing and decolonization."

Waiwhero

Waiwhero is a Maori word that has many meanings, beginning with a creation story.

> *Long ago, before the world was bathed in light, Papatu-anuku, our beloved earth mother, lay cradled within the dark caress of Te Po [the great darkness]. . . . Papatuanuku ripened, growing mountains and valleys, streams and gullies. As she flourished, heavy and wild within the darkness, a new kind of river was born. A deep red river, a bloodied wise moon, carrying dreams of children not yet born. . . .*

Waiwhero is the name of the mythic river of creation and the substance that connects all Maori women back to the original female deities (*atua*). The celebration of a girl's first period is also called *Waiwhero*, when wisdom and responsibility are passed to a new generation and older women tell the new menstruant, "My wellspring of child-bearing has diminished but yours has begun."

Scholar-artist Ngāhuia Murphy's book *Waiwhero: He Whakahirahiratanga o te Ira Wahine* (*The Red Waters: A Celebration of Womanhood*), is an introduction to a menstrual birthright that is being revived among New Zealand's Indigenous people.

Murphy describes a culture where boys and girls learned about menstruation together, where mothers and aunties taught girls how to care for themselves during "their time," and where men cared for menstruating women by gathering special foods, making meals, and giving gifts. Menarche was celebrated with singing, chanting, feasting, and gifts. In some communities, girls were given new adult names; elsewhere there was a ceremonial cutting of hair, ear-piercing, or receiving the traditional women's chin tattoo (*moko kauae*).

Western explorers, settlers, and colonizers dismissed, demonized, and suppressed Maori practices. And although nineteenth- and twentieth-century anthropologists and ethnographers wrote about Indigenous pregnancy and birth rituals, they almost never mentioned menstruation. In 1904, physician and amateur ethnographer W. H. Goldie wrote that there was no special initiation or rite of passage for girls; Murphy suggests the omission might be due to the Western/male aversion to the subject or perhaps Maori women chose not to talk about something so personal to *Pakeha* (non-Maori) men.

Murphy's book is not a history of a bygone ritual but a guide for girls to make it their own. She encourages people to personalize the tradition with suggestions that range from traditional (family feasts and gifts of jewelry made of Maori jade) to contemporary (bubble baths and writing in a journal). She also connects personal observance with the Maori reverence for *Papatuanuku* (Mother Earth), suggesting a quiet walk through the woods or on a beach and making a set of reusable cloth pads for menstruation "because it is better for *Papatuanuku*."

Her goal is for girls to "create *tikanga* (a practice) that's *tika* (correct) for you and your *whanau* (family) for today."

Like Cutcha Risling Baldy and other Indigenous activists, Murphy believes that revitalizing menarche rituals is both a way to promote health and self-esteem in girls and an act of cultural resistance and survival. "If we reclaim menstruation and speak to it as our ancestors did, as a symbol of our continuity, then menstruation becomes an activist site that represents the continued survival of Maori."

The Women's House

The idea of sending menstruating women to live apart from the community is often associated with horror stories of isolation in crude, dangerous hovels (see page 16). But there are cultures where menstrual separation is a comfort and a welcome respite shared with others, a place very reminiscent of a certain fictional red tent.

In the Kalasha tribe—a small ethnic group in northern Pakistan—menstruating women gather in the *bashali*, a large communal house. The Kalasha, who practice an ancient polytheistic religion, consider the *bashali* a "most holy place," where women also give birth and conduct purification ceremonies and ritual offerings.

Anthropologist Wynne Maggi was permitted to visit the *bashali*, where as many as twenty women spend their days taking care of one another and sharing responsibility for children too young to leave at home. In her book, *Our Women Are Free: Gender and Ethnicity in the Hindukush*, Maggi reports that within the confines of the *bashali*, Kalasha women would speak frankly about everything: their marriages, family feuds, and their sex lives. Unmarried girls shared plans for elopement or sought advice about avoiding arranged marriages. Maggi writes: "It is a place women feel free to

behave in ways they ordinarily don't," such as sleeping late, drink-
ing tea, and taking naps. "Life in the *Bashali*," writes Maggi, "re-
minded me of an ongoing slumber party."

For the people of the rain forest who live in the Congo Basin,* the
women's house—the *elima* house—is in the center of the village.
It is the largest structure, and where girls reaching menarche are
welcomed as "blessed by the moon."

    Girls live in the house for weeks, apart but not isolated from
the community; in fact, they bring girlfriends to be taught the skills
and crafts they will need as adult women. They also learn about
sex and motherhood, and women's songs, including a special one
for the *elima* ceremony, which lasts for days. Part of the preparation
includes a "hunting" game, where girls chase boys with sapling
sticks; if a girl lands a blow, the boy has to try to sneak into the
elima, which is guarded by grown women who are intent on keeping him out.

    News of the culminating celebration is shared and people who
live outside the girl's village come for the festivities. Music perme-
ates daily life among the people of the rain forest; the *elima* song
is complex, polyphonic, and especially beautiful. (A recording is
available on YouTube.) Colin Turnbull, an anthropologist who lived
among the Mbuti tribe, described the song in his book *The Forest
People*. "Day after day, night after night, the *elima* house resounds
with the throaty contralto of the older women and the high, pip-
ing voices of the younger." In other songs, the girls sing "a light
cascading melody in intricate harmony, the men replying with a

---

* People of these tribes are widely known as Pygmies, a non-Native term that refers to the short stature of the people but has racist connotations.

rich vital chorus . . . the *elima* is one of the happiest, most joyful occasions in their lives."

The Flower Dance and *Waiwhero, bashali,* and *elima* connect menstruation with joy, respect, and celebration. Learning about indigenous cultures where periods are as natural as the change of the seasons is like opening a window in a dark room.

Shame is not required of us.

New Traditions

Changing the narrative about menstruation from curse to blessing is a tall order. How do you celebrate something that is, for the most part, still hushed up, ignored, and vilified? In the absence of cultural, religious, or family examples, how can a *new* tradition feel authentic?

A tradition is defined as "an inherited, established, or customary pattern of thought, action, or behavior—such as a religious practice or a social custom." That definition might seem to make "new tradition" a contradiction in terms, but in fact, rituals and traditions that survive for centuries are not set in stone; those that pass the test of time change over time. Indigenous women who are studying and reviving menarche customs are not interested in reenacting the old ways for their own sake. Maori writer Ngāhuia Murphy presents the traditional beliefs and practices of her people as a gift for twenty-first-century girls. She writes: "Anyone can assert their own authority and create her own celebratory rituals around *Waiwhero*. To do so is to rescue this symbol from a colonial legacy that has presented it as something 'shameful' and 'dirty.'"

Even cultures that appear to ignore menarche have ceremonies for girls on the brink of adulthood. Bat mitzvah, confirmation, and *quinceañera* all publicly acknowledge the social, spiritual, and intellectual transition from childhood to adulthood; even graduation ceremonies from elementary and middle school are growing-up milestones. Many of these markers occur around the time most girls start menstruating (eleven to thirteen years old). And while menarche is unmentionable where periods are taboo, menstruation is the invisible guest at the party.

There are private or family customs that acknowledge first menstruation: some are long-standing, some are in-the-making; some come with cake and ceremony, and some are acknowledged with little more than a hug.

In Japan, when a girl gets her period, family members are invited for dinner and served a dish called Sekihan. No announcement is made, but once that special preparation of red rice appears on the table, everyone understands that a milestone has been reached.

Regina* who grew up in an extended Sephardic—Mediterranean Jewish—family in the US, remembers that a few days after her first period, her grandmother invited her to afternoon tea. Her mother, aunts, and older girl cousins attended, and the table was set with home-baked cookies—including her favorites.

"I don't remember anyone actually talking about it," she says. "But I knew, and things changed after that. Before, my cousins would chase me out of the kitchen when they were doing dishes, laughing and talking. After I got my period, I was allowed to stay.

"It sounds funny to be happy about doing dishes. But that was where the action was, and now I was part of it."

---

* Pseudonym.

* * *

In some households, menarche is acknowledged by a few words at the dinner table, a special meal, a little gift, or a glass of sparkling grape juice. Grown-ups may get misty-eyed about the passing of time; the honoree may roll their eyes.

Some mothers choose to make menarche a joyful memory. "[It] was a big day in our house. It was the only time my mom allowed me and my two sisters to take the day off of school. We would start out with a special morning together at the house, lounging around. . . . We then went out to lunch at a fancy restaurant and proceeded to an afternoon of shopping to buy a new outfit for the new young woman. . . .

"What I cherish most about the day, though, was spending time with my mom and her talking about how this was a special time that should be celebrated."

Some mothers throw dinner parties for their daughters, inviting the grown women who have been part of her life to share their memories. Women's groups of all affiliations have created a variety of menarche rituals, from church-based ceremonies to an informal circle voicing hopes and wishes for the future.

Then, there is "the slap." Nobody knows when it started, and there is absolutely no basis for it in Jewish law, but it has long been customary for Jewish mothers to slap their daughters when they get their first period.

Rabbi Elyse Goldstein writes: "My mother explained that when she got her period, her mother slapped her and said, 'Welcome to the pain of being a woman.'" Goldstein's mother only tapped her on one cheek and then gave her a kiss on the other.

As a rabbinical student, Goldstein searched Jewish sources for a blessing for menstruation; Judaism supplies a blessing for virtually every human experience, from seeing a rainbow to a healthy bowel movement. Finding none, she created one by turning a troublesome (to say the least) line in the daily morning liturgy, "Blessed are You, Adonai our God . . . who has not made me a woman," to a simple affirmation, "Blessed are You, Adonai our God . . . who has made me a woman."

Says Goldstein: "I wish our tradition had thought of this centuries ago. But it didn't, so we must think it up ourselves."

Goldstein's translation/transformation of that blessing is of a piece with profound changes in Jewish women's roles and rituals. For example, the meaning and practice of immersion after menstruation is used not only by married heterosexual couples but also by unmarried people, people in same-sex relationships, and people who are not sexually active. To paraphrase Ngāhuia Murphy, women have uncoupled menstruation from a legacy of shame and claimed the authority to find new meaning in old traditions.

Ritual immersion has always been a way to acknowledge important changes in status: from unmarried to married, from not-Jewish to Jewish (conversion). Today, immersion is being used to honor and sanctify transitions of all kinds, including the entire life-cycle of the menstruating body: from menarche to menopause and everything in between—pregnancy, infertility, weaning, illness, and recovery.

A meditation for menarche before immersing

I welcome this stage of Womanhood with a mixture of
emotions.
I don't know what the future will bring or how this great change
in my body
will bring changes to other parts of my life. May I always respect
my body and the potential it holds.

A meditation for menopause before immersing

A season is set for everything, a time for every
experience under heaven.
A time of flow and time of stillness,
A time of ending and a time of beginning
A time for menstruation and a time for menopause.

New traditions are experiments.

Some will wither away, others will stick, and, after a few generations, new menstruators will come to expect the same kind of party/ceremony/gift as their parents and grandparents. Given the creativity and boldness of young menstrual activists today, there is bound to be an abundance of original and surprising experiments to come.

PART THREE

The Struggle

Even in the best of cases—access to period products, running water, privacy, and health care—menstruation is not (pick your cliché) a picnic, a walk in the park, or a piece of cake.

Without access to products, running water, privacy, or health care, menstruation is a problem, a burden, a nightmare, a crisis, a violation of human rights, and a miserable fact of life for millions. The struggle against menstrual injustice is being waged on multiple fronts: fighting taxes that are levied only on menstruators; organizing to change unhealthy and unsafe workplace conditions; advocating for menstruators who are imprisoned, homeless, or stateless; exposing the systemic racism that puts people of color at risk to a disproportionate extent; and challenging the treatment of menstruators with disabilities.

Period Poverty and the Tampon Tax

Period poverty wears many faces.

It's Sunday night and you're at the kitchen table with the checkbook. The bills are paid but there's only $50 to last until Friday. It'll be tight, but just enough to cover bus fare and milk and stuff to make chili or soup. It's good the little ones get breakfast and lunch at school.

Then your oldest walks in with an empty tampon box.

*

It's Monday morning and you lie in bed thinking about the day ahead: math test, track team tryout. I could stuff a wad of toilet paper in my underwear, which means worrying all day: Is it going to leak? Will it fall out? The last time I asked the school nurse for a pad, she was all out and I really don't want to ask my friends—again.

No softball tryouts for me. Maybe I can keep it together through math. Or maybe I should just stay home.

Menstrual products are expensive. According to one estimate, menstruators spend $17,000 during their lifetime, a figure that includes pads, tampons, panty liners, pain medication, and underwear; but a number that doesn't account for higher prices paid in poor neighborhoods, where people lack easy access to supermarkets or drugstores. Period poverty exists in every country, every state, every zip code. Period poverty is not the same for everyone: it can mean an empty tampon box or nowhere to dry your cloth pads; it can mean no clean water to wash your hands, no toilets to take care of yourself in private, and no way to dispose of what you used.

Period poverty means counting pennies to come up with something as basic as toilet paper, and it can make you miss school or work, which can lose you your job if it happens once too often. Period poverty can mean failing math, or getting put in detention, or maybe you should just quit school altogether. It's a weight, a doubt, a nagging worry that makes you feel out of control, or hopeless, or like a bad mother.

Period poverty is compounded by "the tampon tax," a somewhat misleading term since there is no special tax on tampons, pads, or other period products. It's an umbrella term that covers different kinds of levies: state and city sales taxes, value-added taxes, and even luxury taxes. Whoever collects the money, the tax is paid only by people who menstruate.

In the United States, sales tax in most states ranges from 4 to 7 percent, though in 2020, Alabama, Arkansas, Louisiana, and Tennessee hovered around 9 percent. The addition of ninety cents to a ten-dollar box of tampons makes a difference if your food budget is already stretched to the limit.

Some employers in the US offer their workers the option of setting aside a portion of their pay in a Health Savings Account or a Flexible Spending Account. That money, which is not taxed as income, can be used for medical expenses and over-the-counter items, such as antacids, sunscreen, and birth control methods including condoms. But not period products.

So if you have an HSA or an FSA and need tampons, you paid with money that was taxed as income and again through sales tax. It took the COVID-19 emergency for Congress to amend the rules to include tampons, pads, liners, and cups in the pre-tax category.

People who depend on federal assistance programs (SNAP/food stamps or WIC/women with children) cannot use their benefits for period products, which with toilet paper and diapers are the three most requested items and rarely donated items at shelters and food pantries.

Jennifer Weiss-Wolf, the author of *Periods Gone Public* and co-founder of the advocacy organization Period Equity, says the tax on period products is sex-based discrimination, unconstitutional, and illegal.

An attorney, Weiss-Wolf is leading the charge to get rid of period taxes in all fifty states. She dismisses the argument that repealing taxes on period products would punch big holes in state budgets and asks why revenue should come only from people who menstruate when there are hundreds of exemptions on items that are gender-neutral and utterly nonessential: there is no sales tax on Mardi Gras beads in Louisiana, Texas doesn't tax candy bars, and several states exempt snack foods altogether.

However, things are getting better.

In 2015, only ten states exempted period products—and five of those had no sales tax to begin with. By 2020, twenty states had abolished the tampon tax, with campaigns to do the same in the other thirty. Some cities—Denver, Chicago, and Washington, DC—have eliminated local taxes on period products.

There are campaigns to end taxes on period products all over the world, thanks to public pressure, media attention, and the growing presence of women in office at all levels. Kenya was the first country to abolish them in 2004. Australia, Canada, Colombia,

India, Ireland, Malaysia, Malta, Rwanda, and Scotland have since followed suit.

As Weiss-Wolf writes in *Periods Gone Public*, "In order to have a fully equitable society, we must have laws and policies that take into account the reality that half the population menstruates. Menstrual products should be tax-exempt, affordable and available for all, safe for our bodies and the planet."

In answer to the inevitable question about cost, Nancy Kramer, founder of the Free the Tampons Foundation, says, "Whoever pays for the toilet paper, pays for the pads."

Kramer is an advocate for "restroom equality" and had a hand in getting New York City to provide free period products to public school students in grades six to twelve. Two years later, the State of New York extended that mandate to all school districts in the state.

Free period products are starting to show up in public bathrooms, with sightings in hotels, restaurants, museums, co-working spaces, retail stores, and corporate offices. College students on every continent are demanding them, and for the most part succeeding.

Scotland is the world leader on the accessibility front. In 2018, after a yearslong grassroots campaign, it began requiring all schools, colleges, and universities to provide free pads and tampons. And in 2020, the Scottish parliament unanimously passed the Period Products Act, which designated funding for localities to provide them to anyone in need nationwide.

Only fools make predictions, but the dual campaigns to end the tampon tax and to provide free products in public restrooms are at a turning point, which is more of a likelihood than an inflection point. A turning point is what happens when you look around the corner and see your destination up ahead.

Menstruating
at Work

M *an may work from sun to sun*—a woman's work is never done. Regardless of her menstrual status.

Women—all but the most privileged—haven't stopped working since Eve and Adam got evicted from Eden. In scorching heat and numbing cold, in good health, sick as a dog, menstruating or lactating, women have never been off the clock. When historians talk about women "entering the workforce" during the industrial revolution, World War II, or after publication of Betty Friedan's book *The Feminine Mystique*—they ignore and erase the work of hearth and home: raising crops and caring for animals, preparing food and serving it and cleaning up afterward, making clothes and goods to sell or trade: candles, soap, tamales, or other home goods; also childcare, eldercare, everyone care, and doing all the laundry. Or what the International Labor Organization (ILO) calls "unpaid care work."

Just under half (47.7 percent) of all women on the planet worked outside the home in 2019 compared to nearly 75 percent of men; and whether or not women work outside the home, they are responsible for 75 percent of all the unpaid care work.

A 2019 US Bureau of Labor Statistics report showed that

93 percent of men with children under the age of eighteen were part of the workforce; 72 percent were women—most of whom (62 percent) had children under the age of four.

There are two ways to look at these numbers. While it might seem as if men (as a group) work more than women, that view ignores the fact that women put in many more uncounted hours of unpaid care work, whether or not they have terrible cramps, access to a bathroom, or enough pads or tampons to get through the day.

For women in the workforce, talking about the challenge of menstruation on the job has been taboo, not only because it is embarrassing (another word for shameful) but also because any mention of periods—especially any distress—could make you look like an unreliable employee, or even an example of why women are biologically less suited to participating in the workforce.

Given the risk, women rarely speak up about what they need—much less what they deserve. During the early days of the global coronavirus pandemic, doctors and nurses who cared for the sick and contagious were extravagantly praised as heroes for working endless hours and putting their own health and safety at risk. When the epidemic reached crisis proportions in the Wuhan province city of Hubai, female medical workers—by far the majority—ran out of menstrual supplies. A twenty-one-year-old nurse took to the internet and reported that when she and her colleagues asked supervisors to buy disposable period underwear, they were told to "deal with it themselves."

When Shanghai resident Jiang Jinjing saw that, she forwarded the message and launched a donation drive that sent hundreds of thousands of pads and period underwear to China. Some hospital administrators turned away the donations, either unaware or dismissive of the need. Eventually, the supplies arrived, but not before the story was widely reported, eliciting outrage and adding another crack in the wall of silence that keeps menstruation a secret for no good reason.

There are places where menstruation is an occupational health hazard. Women comprise 90 percent of the nearly 40 million people employed by Bangladesh's garment industry; although wages are low and working conditions are generally poor and often dangerous, the jobs are prized because there are few other opportunities for women to support themselves and their families.

Change Associates, a nonprofit organization that works to empower and educate women garment workers in Bangladesh, conducted a health survey of workers in 2010. Seventy percent of those who responded reported symptoms such as vaginal stinging and rashes. With limited bathroom breaks, and unable to afford manufactured products, women resorted to stuffing handfuls of "joot" into their underwear; joot is the leftover scraps of fabric that get swept into corners of the factory floor. It itches, is difficult to keep in place, prone to leaking, and, given the dirt and the toxic chemicals used in some fabrics, is the likely cause of widespread genitourinary problems.

The fact that this small study, which lacks academic standing, is still widely cited, speaks to another problem. "There is no research into how menstruators are affected by not being able to manage their periods in a functioning pattern in their working lives," writes Anna Dahlqvist in her book, *It's Only Blood*. "Studies about access to toilets, water, and bathroom breaks from a menstrual perspective are conspicuous by their absence."

Factory work brings people together, which allows for the possibility of collective action and representation. Manufacturers in

Dhaka began to provide subsidized period products in the bathrooms, not so much because it benefited the women, but because Change Associates convinced business owners they would lower the high absentee rate that was hurting their bottom line.

Applying collective pressure is nearly impossible for many of the world's agricultural laborers who, unlike factory workers, tend to be isolated. According to the United Nations International Labor Organization, agriculture is one of the three most dangerous occupations on earth, and one of the lowest paid.

Saanvi is a farmworker who lives in the central Indian district of Beed. When she was thirty-six years old, she went to the doctor complaining of cramps, white discharge, and a foul smell. She was told that her uterus was damaged and "hysterectomy was the way out." Saanvi* already had two children and didn't want more, and since the operation would mean an end to periods, she agreed. That made her the seventh woman in her family to have her uterus removed in a village where as many as 50 percent of women have had the operation.

Every year, hundreds of thousands of Beed residents migrate to neighboring areas to work as sugarcane cutters. Contractors hire couples as a single unit—*ek koyta* "one sickle"—to cut and load as much as five thousand pounds of cane in a sixteen-hour day, which begins at six in the morning, though women rise at four a.m. to prepare food for the family.

If a couple misses their quota, they are fined, and so are contractors. According to one of these middlemen, "We have a target to complete in a limited time frame and hence we don't want a woman who would have periods during cane cutting." He insists

---

* Pseudonym.

families make their own choice about surgery, but women have reported that some contractors provide an advance to pay for the operation and then garnish the family wages to repay the loan.

There is also data that implicates local physicians. Between 2016 and 2019, approximately 6,600 hysterectomies were performed in Beed: 4,605 in private hospitals, 2,000 in public hospitals. The numbers raised alarm bells. Doctors affiliated with the private hospitals deny any wrongdoing and claim they are being scapegoated for conditions beyond their control, such as early marriage and childbirth, and poor hygiene. But after the government required all gynecologists to seek permission from a civil surgeon before performing any but emergency hysterectomies, the number of procedures in the region decreased by 50 percent.

Saanvi's doctor said that the operation would put an end to her symptoms but never mentioned possible side effects, like the back and joint pain that kept her in bed for three months after the surgery. "On many days, the pain is unbearable," she says. "It's like I have aged at a greater speed."

The medical establishment has been wrong about menstruation—wittingly and unwittingly—for a very long time. In the late nineteenth and early twentieth centuries, doctors warned that the strain of riding a bicycle or going to college was too much for women to handle, especially while on their periods. In the 1960s, as women started to enter the workforce in large numbers, premenstrual syndrome (PMS) became the source of a thousand jokes about how women became irrational and overemotional, unable to control the urge to eat ice cream or drop nuclear bombs—pretty much the same baloney ascribed to menopause.

In 1964, Patsy Mink, then a newly elected member of the US House of Representatives from Hawaii, was quoted saying, "I wouldn't see anything wrong with a woman president."

Dr. Edgar Berman disagreed. "Suppose that we had a menopausal woman president who had to make the decision on the Bay of Pigs or the Russian contretemps with Cuba?" said Berman, a member of the Democratic Party's Committee on National Priorities. She might be "subject to the curious mental aberration of that age group."

Mink wasn't having it. "His use of the menstrual cycle and menopause to ridicule women and to caricature all women as neurotic and emotionally unbalanced was ... indefensible and astonishing."

Dr. Berman called Mink's response "a typical example of an ordinarily controlled woman under the raging hormonal imbalance of the periodical lunar cycle." Soon thereafter, the doctor "resigned" from the committee with a whine, saying, "The whole world seems to be uptight."

The whole world went on to elect at least forty-six women heads of state, beginning with Indira Gandhi in 1966.

Fifty-one years after Dr. Berman's remarks, Donald Trump gave voice to the old menstrual libel after TV anchor Megyn Kelly prefaced a debate question to the then-candidate by saying, "You've called women you don't like fat pigs, dogs, slobs, and disgusting animals." Denying nothing, he smirked that he'd only used those words to describe one particular woman.

Later, when asked about this exchange, Trump said that Kelly had, "Blood coming out of her eyes. Blood coming out of her wherever."

Jaws dropped, but when he was called on it, Trump claimed he was talking about blood "coming out of her nose" and anyone who thought otherwise had "a dirty mind."

* * *

Given that the millions who menstruate daily are exceptionally skilled at keeping that fact a deep dark secret, a well-intentioned public effort to shed light on it created a minor firestorm in 2019 when a Japanese department store requested that saleswomen consider wearing a "Little Miss Period" badge when they were menstruating.

Little Miss Period—Seiri-chan—is the heroine of an award-winning manga series by Ken Koyama. Seiri-chan is a walking cartoon uterus that visits menstruating women every month and punches them in the gut with painful cramps, but she's not all bad; in one issue she travels back in time to visit Yoshiko Sakai, the woman who produced the first commercial menstrual pads sold in Japan.

When Little Miss Period became the star of a live-action movie—played by a life-size stuffed animal—the Daimaru department store opened a new boutique department selling Seiri-chan merchandise, clothing, and period products—something they had never sold before. That was when the Seiri-chan badges appeared on the lapels of menstruating salespeople.

The store went on the defense; no one was required to wear the badge, nor were they intended to let customers know anyone's menstrual status. Their purpose was only to encourage co-workers to be more considerate and offer to help lifting heavy objects.

The badges were scrapped. Or as the company put it, "re-thought." Menstruation does not cause upper body weakness. However, up to 20 percent of women suffer from dysmenor-rhea: cramps, headaches, dizziness, nausea, and diarrhea severe enough to interfere with normal activities for a few days. For most employed menstruators who have those symptoms, options are limited: call in sick and use one of a limited number of sick days; lose a day's pay or risk getting fired; or go to work and tough it out as best you can. The other—still rare—possibility is menstrual leave, where employees can take paid or unpaid days off without prejudice.

Japan implemented a menstrual leave policy in 1947, when the country needed women workers to join a workforce decimated by the war, but the idea was not widely adopted. Fifty-plus years later, other Asian nations followed suit: South Korea in 2001, Indonesia in 2003, and Taiwan in 2014. But because those laws are rarely enforced, employers have largely ignored them, and women rarely ask for time off for fear of losing their jobs.

There are a few examples of successful government-mandated leave. The Indian state Bihar has provided two days of monthly menstrual leave since 1992, apparently without incident. Zambia passed a "Mother's Day" law in 2016, guaranteeing a monthly day off for all women, whether or not they are mothers and whether or not they are menstruating. The rationale for calling it "Mother's Day" was to acknowledge the caregiving work done almost exclusively by women, which is laudable although it assumes men do not now nor ever will have family obligations and responsibilities.

Some women have managed to create their own personal time-out. Jeanette MacDonald, a Hollywood star of the 1920s and '30s, had a clause in her contract that allowed her days off for menstruation like many other actresses. This benefit was not public knowledge, but Clark Gable knew and he grumbled about having to work when his hemorrhoids were acting up.

Menstrual leave is a contentious idea.

On March 8, 2020, International Women's Day, Shashi Tharoor, a member of the Indian parliament, posted an online petition proposing national laws so that "all employed women in India should have an option to take 'work from home' or 'leave with pay for two days every month, by private and public employers.'" It cited Article 42 of the Indian constitution: "The State shall make provision for securing just and humane conditions of work and for maternity relief."

The backlash was furious. Journalist Barkha Dutt reprised a fiery opinion piece she'd written for the *Washington Post* years earlier, calling the idea "a bizarrely paternalistic and silly proposal to further ghettoize us." She wrote that period leave "may be dressed up as progressive, but it actually trivializes the feminist agenda for equal opportunity, especially in male-dominated professions. Worse, it reaffirms that there is a biological determinism to the lives of women. . . . Remember all those dumb jokes by male colleagues about 'that time of the month'?"

A number of small-to-medium-size businesses and nonprofits have instituted a monthly day off or allowed menstruating workers to work from home, but menstrual leave is still such an outlier among larger companies that the international press was all over the news that Zomato, one of India's largest food-delivery firms, had instituted ten days of leave a year for its four thousand employees, 35 percent of whom are women.

Feminists are divided on the question of menstrual leave; some view it as progressive and inclusive, others reject it as regressive and a threat to gains women have made. Professor Elizabeth Hill, who studies menstrual leave at the University of Sydney in Australia, notes a generational divide in the debate: "It's almost as if the over-40s are horrified by the idea while, anecdotally, a lot of the younger women are like, 'yah, that's a great idea.'"

Hill says that the conversation about menstrual leave raises a much more fundamental question. "It challenges the notion of the 'ideal worker' who is *care-less* and *body-less*." In other words, as interchangeable as widgets.

To date, the rules about work have been written by and for men who have few (if any) caregiving responsibilities, and whose bodies do not regularly change over the course of a month. Also to date, the struggle for gender equality at work has required women to act as though they do not have periods. In the paradigm that worker = male, menstrual leave consigns women to a separate or inferior status—it makes them a problem.

When the happy day arrives when everyone agrees that (1) women are people and (2) workers are not robots but human beings with bodies and souls, the workplace will be reconfigured to provide safe bathrooms with free period products and the means for their disposal—also baby-changing stations and accommodations for people with disabilities.

But the more-essential change goes far beyond the bathroom. Treating all workers as human beings requires generous sick leave, work-at-home options, and paid personal days so that nobody is penalized for taking time off for a menstrual migraine or to bring a sick child to the doctor.

Dignity

If the famous "arc of justice" is moving to abolish all obstacles that keep human beings from the pursuit of happiness, then menstrual justice has to be part of that great and worthy goal for everyone and every body, including those with disabilities.

People with disabilities of all kinds and degrees have often been treated as sub-human or as perpetual children and excluded from making decisions that affect every aspect of their lives. Parents and other caregivers routinely have withheld information about menstruation and sexuality from young women with disabilities as they matured, in a misguided attempt to "protect" them.

In many cases, caregivers had periods suppressed altogether—either chemically or surgically—a choice sometimes based on their own discomfort, exhaustion, and fear, without including the menstruator in the decision, regardless of their ability to participate.

In 2016, after years of work by disability rights advocates, the American Academy of Pediatrics and the American College of Obstetricians and Gynecologists issued policies seeking to ensure the participation of people with disabilities in health-care choices to the greatest extent possible. So, for example, if a caregiver requests menstrual suppression for a child because of their own inability to deal with menses or because they are fearful of sexual abuse, health-care providers are advised to investigate further and help families explore other choices. Advocates and caregivers also encourage connecting young people with disabled adults, who can act as mentors and share their feelings and strategies about periods, which are as diverse as those of people without disabilities: from "I hate it. If I could make it stop I would" to "Menstruation is a nice reminder that something is 'working normally' in my body."

Race Matters

"The older black women in my life often made me feel bad about my period," writes Tiffanie Woods. "Things like reproductive health and mental illness have always held stereotypes in the black community, leading to shaming instead of educating and denying instead of embracing.

"But it's not their fault," Woods continues. "The way the black community treats menstruation stems from decades of internalized racism and classism."

Systemic racism has wreaked havoc on the health of Black people in America; Black women are two to three times more likely to die of pregnancy-related causes and Black women have the highest mortality rate (30 percent) of any group in the United States. Black women are also less likely to be diagnosed with fibroids or endometriosis, even though fibroids are more common among Black women, and even when diagnosed, they are less likely to receive pain medication.

Medicine is not color-blind.

In a 2016 survey of 222 medical students and residents, as many as half agreed with one or more of the following statements:

- "Black people's nerve endings are less sensitive than white people's."

- "Black people's skin is thicker than white people's."

- "Black people's blood coagulates more quickly than white people's."

The American Medical Association acknowledged the problem in 2003: "Neither the health care system as a whole nor individual providers are fully insulated from attitudes toward race, ethnicity, and social class that are prevalent (though often unacknowledged) in the larger society."

American medicine's history of racism goes back nearly as far as the medical system itself. James Marion Sims (1813–1883), a physician and surgeon often called the "father of modern gynecology," practiced surgical techniques on enslaved Black women without anesthesia in the 1800s. The infamous Tuskegee study, where Black men were given placebos rather than penicillin to treat syphilis, did not end until 1972, *a year within living memory.*

This appalling record echoes through countless personal experiences of disrespect, neglect, and worse and has fostered a generalized distrust of the medical establishment. And because this history of negative experiences keeps people from seeking preventive care, it puts them at increased health risks.

A recent study showed that Black patients receive better care from Black primary care doctors, in large part because of better communication and trust. Dr. Magdala Chery, an internist, recounts an experience familiar to female physicians of color. "Black women will come and say, 'Oh great, now I can ask you a question because I've been so uncomfortable asking my other doctor.'" Unfortunately, the chances are slim for a Black woman to get an appointment with an ob-gyn who looks like her: only 11 percent of ob-gyns are Black.

Dr. Charis Chambers, an ob-gyn who specializes in the management of periods for teens and young adults, has had that same experience many times over. Chambers spends a lot of time dispelling myths and misconceptions she hears from patients, something she does both in her clinical practice and online as The Period Doctor. "The most beautiful experience when I see patients is to counsel cross-generationally," says Dr. Chambers. "The daughter might say 'I didn't know that,' and then the mother or grandmother will also say 'I didn't know that.' Learning together makes other kinds of conversations possible."

Tiffanie Woods writes: "Black people's feelings of self-worth have long been tied to our appearances: how 'clean' we are, and nothing is seen as more 'dirty' than period blood."

Bria Gadsden of Love Your Menses (see page 32) says the goal of her organization is "to teach girls to understand their bodies, to know how to take care of themselves, and to replace fear with confidence," a mission that extends from Boston to partnerships with groups serving girls around the US and in Africa. The Black Women's Health Imperative, the Association of Black Women Physicians, and the White Dress Project are among the organizations challenging menstrual stigma in the Black community and institutional racism in medicine.

The medical community has documented and acknowledged racial discrimination within its ranks, conditions that have taken on greater urgency in the wake of the Black Lives Matter movement. And yet, "The medical community largely avoids talking about how systemic racism affects our Black and brown patients individually," writes Harvard Medical School student Ayotomiwa Ojo. "We are more comfortable talking about the social determinants of health for marginalized people, collectively, rather than discussing how we disenfranchise the patient under our care."

Menstruating While Incarcerated

The United States has only 5 percent of the world's female population but more than 30 percent of the world's incarcerated women. More than 200,000 women are incarcerated in American prisons, jails, and juvenile and immigration lockups, where People of Color and nonbinary people are overrepresented by large margins.

All prison systems were built and designed for men, so accommodations for women have always been an afterthought. In 2000, the United Nations enacted a set of seventy regulations for the treatment of women prisoners. Rule Number 5 mandates that all women in custody be supplied with pads or tampons and facilities for bathing.

American compliance with that rule has been inadequate, to put it mildly. The Federal Bureau of Prisons stipulated that period products be "made available," which in practice has mostly meant selling pads and tampons in prison commissaries, which means that some women had to choose between phone calls to their kids or bleeding through their clothes. Furthermore, that rule applied to federal institutions, which accounts for only 7 percent of female-identified prisoners—not the 93 percent who are locked up in state prisons, local jails, or facilities for juveniles. In prisons and jails that do provide/sell period supplies, they are mostly inadequate and shoddy.

Over the past decade, prisoners and advocates have increased efforts to expose the misery of menstruation behind bars, taking their stories to the media and challenging current practices in court. In 2014, a group of prisoners in Michigan filed a lawsuit charging that delays in getting products caused them to bleed through their clothes, which they were forced to wear until the next weekly laundry day. In Connecticut, two women sharing a cell were given five pads per week to share between them.

A 2015 report about conditions in New York State's women's prisons revealed a pattern of systematic humiliation. In one facility, women who requested "extra" pads were screened for anemia to make sure they "really" needed them; at another state prison, the medical director demanded visual evidence of a woman's need for more than the allotted number. He was quoted as saying, "We need her to bring in a bag of used sanitary napkins to show that she actually has used them and needs more."

Chandra Bozelko, a blogger, author, and activist who spent six years in a Connecticut jail, wrote that the experiences of lacking supplies and bleeding through your clothes are "indelible reminders of one's powerlessness in prison, asking for something you need crystalizes the power differential between inmates and guards." Kimberly Haven, another formerly incarcerated prison activist, writes: "Pads and tampons have become weaponized."

In 2012, a complaint was filed with the United States Department of Justice (DOJ) against the Alabama prison system about conditions at the Julia Tutwiler Prison for Women. After two years of study, the DOJ determined that its treatment of women rose to the level of cruel and unusual punishment, which is a violation of the Eighth Amendment to the US Constitution. Tutwiler was called "a toxic environment with repeated and open sexual behavior," including "officers forcing prisoners to engage in sexual acts in exchange for basic sanitary supplies."

In 2017, the Federal Bureau of Prisons (BOP) issued new regulations explicitly requiring that period products be made available to inmates "free of charge" in federal prisons. Again, those rules had no impact on state prisons or any other jail or juvenile facility, which left it up to the states to mandate access to basic human necessities.

Legislators in state houses around the country have been filing legislation to fix this. In 2018, Arizona state representative Athena Salman tried to change the state regulation that mandated exactly twelve free pads (no tampons) per prisoner per month. In her testimony before the legislature, Adrienne Kitcheyan, a former inmate, said, "Bloodstained pants, bartering, and begging for pads and tampons was a regular occurrence." Those bloodstains were not only humiliating, they could result in punishment for breaking the prison's dress code, which was an infraction that could revoke access to the commissary, which is where pads and tampons were sold.

Representative Salman's bill passed a first hearing, but when the chairman of the rules committee refused to move it forward, furious constituents flooded his mailbox with tampons. After that, the Arizona Department of Corrections announced an increase in the allotment of pads from twelve to thirty-six, and stated, "An inmate may request and, without charge, receive additional pads, if necessary."

That may sound like a victory, but the devil is in the language: "may request" means "must request." As for "if necessary," who decides?

In 2019, the American Bar Association adopted a policy urging federal, state, local, territorial, and tribal legislatures to enact legislation, for correctional and detention facilities to provide unlimited free access to toilet paper and menstrual hygiene products (sanitary pads and tampons) to adult and juvenile women prisoners in all forms of detention.

"Passing laws and resolutions may feel good," says Diane Abbate, an attorney who worked in the Civil Rights Division of the Department of Justice during the Tutwiler Prison investigation. "But that's not the solution."

Abbate says the solution lies with the people who implement policies; with the wardens and guards who receive little training, guidance, or support to make essential changes. Unfortunately, investment in staff development is rarely a priority.

"Menstruation is a matter of dignity," says Abbate. "Humiliation is not a constitutional violation. But it should be."

Homeless and Refugee Menstruators

People living on the street and sleeping in shelters, surviving in refugee camps or waiting in immigration lockup, are tired, hungry, and frightened; then they get their period and face nothing but awful choices: beg, borrow, make a pad out of toilet paper, use a sock, or just sit still until it's dark so no one will see the stains.

Sadly, it's not difficult to ignore or forget the millions of refugees who are isolated in camps, hidden behind bars, or even locked in cages. It's harder to disregard the distress of a homeless woman sitting on the sidewalk in front of your laundromat or to forget the face of a woman who approaches you for help.

In its 2020 update, the National Alliance to End Homelessness reported 219,000 homeless women in the United States: Native Americans and Pacific Island women are four times more likely to be homeless than any other racial or ethnic group and 40 percent of homeless youth identify as LGBTQ or nonbinary.

In Canada, mass homelessness emerged as a national problem in the 1980s as a result of disinvestment in affordable housing and reduced support for social services. By 2019, 235,000 Canadians experienced homelessness at some point in the year, though that number is widely considered an undercount. Twenty-seven percent of the homeless are women, of whom up to 75 percent have a mental illness; domestic violence has been cited as a leading cause of the rise in family homelessness.

The largest Canadian homeless population is in Toronto, which is where special education teacher Jana Girdauskas was approached by a homeless woman who needed help. The encounter set Girdauskas to wondering what happened to homeless women when they got their periods. She decided to be ready with material help the next time she was asked for assistance, so she gathered period supplies and other necessities and put them in a purse—so it would feel more like a gift than a handout. She posted on Facebook to see if any of her friends had a spare pocketbook. Within a month Girdauskas had 350 handbags filled with supplies, which she brought to local shelters; within the year she founded The Period Purse to keep the efforts going. High school and church groups joined in, collecting products and assembling them for delivery to organizations that worked with homeless women. The local media ran stories, familiarizing the public with terms like "menstrual stigma" and "period poverty." Within two years, the Toronto City Council allocated funds for period products in shelters and drop-in centers for the first time, and the Toronto public school system began supplying pads and tampons in its middle and high schools.

The Period Purse story is just one example of efforts in Africa, Europe, the US, and elsewhere that often begins when a woman or teenage girl witnesses an example of menstrual humiliation—on the street or from a news story or a documentary—and can't look away. She organizes a drive to collect products and distribute them in her community, starts a nonprofit to keep it going; she becomes an advocate for menstrual justice and is featured in local media, building awareness, support, and empathy.

A few of Period Purse's "sister" organizations include: Flo Code, Austin, Texas; #happyperiod.org, Los Angeles, California; Helping Women Period, Lansing, Michigan; The Homeless Period Project, Greenville, South Carolina; I Support the Girls, Wheaton, Maryland; Free Periods, United Kingdom; Inua Dada Foundation, Kenya; Myna Mahila Foundation, India; Once-a-Month, South Africa.

While some groups remain focused on providing products where needed, many take on a much larger project. The Period Purse's mission is "to reduce the stigma of menstruation through public education and by advocating for menstrual-equity policies in Toronto and throughout Canada." And as it says on its website, its goal is nothing less than "to disrupt the existing system."

no one leaves home unless home is the mouth of a shark . . .
no one leaves home unless home chases you
                                    —from "Home," a poem by Warsan Shire

According to the United Nations Refugee Agency (UNHCR), 37,000 people left their homes every day in 2018 because of conflict, persecution, or environmental disaster—more than at any other point in recorded history. UNHCR estimates that there were more than 70 million displaced people in the world; 35 million of them women and girls.

There are few more miserable places to menstruate than in a refugee camp. Tents are crowded, cots are shared, access to water is limited. There are no locks on the toilets, no bins to dispose of pads. If you're lucky enough to have a kit with wipes and a reusable pad, there's no hook to hang it on and the floor is filthy. Going to the toilet at night puts women at risk of sexual assault.

This perfect storm of indignities violates the 2018 United Nations Human Rights Council statement about Menstrual Health Management (MHM), which calls upon all countries to provide clean water, menstrual health education, and to "address the widespread stigma and shame surrounding menstruation and menstrual hygiene . . . and ensuring universal access to hygienic products and gender-sensitive facilities, including disposal options for menstrual products."

The goal is more honored in the breach than in the observance.

The United States operates the world's largest immigration detention system but ranks fiftieth among nations that admit refugees. In the summer of 2019, conditions in detention centers on the US–Mexico border made international headlines with pictures of children in custody in cramped quarters—including cages—sleeping on the floor and getting sick. A complaint filed by nineteen states against the Department of Homeland Security included testimony from teenage girls who said they were given only one pad a day while menstruating and denied a change of clothes.

And then there was the story about a young girl, separated from her family, who had bled through her clothes and been forced to sit in her own menstrual blood.

Even though her name was never mentioned and there were no photographs, the mental image broke through the compassion fatigue of a world overwhelmed by disasters and suffering. The story about the stain was reported and repeated for several days and remains a touchstone for outrage against America's refugee policies and menstrual humiliation.

That unnamed teenage girl had been stripped of her ability

to uphold the universal expectation that she hide it, deny it, and pretend it wasn't happening. It was a kind of nakedness that had been forced upon her, and while she doubtlessly felt ashamed, the shame was not hers: it was America's.

Marni Sommer, professor at the Columbia University Mailman School of Public Health and a prolific MHM researcher and advocate, writes about the importance of changing the way the world thinks about menstrual injustice, of "reframing" it, so that what has always been considered a private matter or a cultural inevitability becomes "an immoral reality" and "a concern that can be shared and acted upon."

Reframing menstrual dignity as a human right may sound uncontroversial, but in fact it represents a change as radical as the "discovery" that the sun, moon, and planets did not, in fact, revolve around the Earth.

PART FOUR

Menstruation Goes Public

Men are talking and writing about periods—as parents, allies, and advocates. Corporations are increasingly willing to call a tampon a tampon. Women-owned companies are creating new period products and selling them with humor and appeals to universal sisterhood. Nonprofits committed to menstrual justice continue to proliferate and spread the word, as do advocacy groups sounding the alarm about environmental hazards and health-safety risks.

Silence and secrecy persist, but the taboo is fading.

Men-struation

I t has been possible—easy, actually—for boys to grow into manhood with virtually no knowledge of menstruation. And it's not their fault.

Women, schooled in fifty shades of shame, have kept the bleeding out of sight. If there was a slip—a tampon box left out on a bathroom counter, an overheard comment about a heavy flow, or, God forbid, a bloodstain—it was understood that a woman had failed to maintain the unspoken understanding that This. Was. Not. Happening.

This protocol has permitted a thousand misconceptions to flourish. In 1983, when Sally Ride prepared to become the first American woman astronaut, the NASA engineers asked whether a hundred tampons would be enough for her ten-day trip in space.

No surprise, then, that when @brownandbella asked followers to post the dumbest thing a man had ever said to them about periods, she got two thousand responses, including:

- He said tampons are sex toys.

- He said my periods were long and painful because I didn't drink enough water.

- Someone I was dating asked if I could reschedule my period so it wouldn't coincide with his birthday. We didn't make it to his birthday.

- He asked me if I got sad every time I had a period because every period is a dead baby.

- He thought women literally expelled an egg—roughly the size of a small Cadbury egg—during every period.

- He asked me why don't we push it all out at once instead of "Waiting for it to fall out" over seven days.

- My husband of almost thirteen years says "Again?" every time I start my period.

There were some ugly responses, too, like the report of a father who beat his daughter when he learned she had started her period because he thought menstruation was brought on by having sex. And from a woman who said that her former partner, a medical student, screamed and kicked her out of his dormitory when she bled after sex. He said "that can only happen when you have an STD." He later sent her a Facebook message, accusing her of giving him AIDS.

Misogyny, nonsense, and squeamishness are not going to disappear anytime soon, but they are treatable conditions. Given the opportunity, men and boys will admit to confusion and embarrassment, ask for information, express outrage at menstrual injustice, and even laugh at themselves.

YKA (Voice of Youth), a youth social media platform in India, hosted a writing contest, "Period Path," asking for "an open letter to your government representative for better menstrual hygiene facilities."

Not all of the letters came from women.

S.P. wrote: "My school never gave us a session on menstrual hygiene. Girls were given different 'workshops,' but we were not told about it. This led to very dizzy concepts," which made him sound insensitive and rude, "like a period criminal." S.P. resorted to Google for help, "which led to very wrong and half-baked information."

He concluded that the problem was "the whole education system," and that menstruation should be a mandatory subject "for all."

"The whole education system" in much of the world has mostly failed miserably at communicating the basics about human biology, and periods hardly at all. But learning how things work is not the same as understanding what it's like to live in a body that's different from your own. According to frontline teachers and the professional literature on sexual-health education, that requires teaching students of all genders in the same room, at the same time.

Separating boys and girls for sex-ed has been standard for decades. But separate is not equal. In segregated classes, boys tend not to learn about menstruation and period shame, girls don't hear about wet dreams, and everyone gets the message that whatever "they" are learning is off-limits and is nothing "we" need to know. For transgender and nonbinary kids, separate tracks keep them from information they need perhaps more than anyone else; it can also force them to lie about their identity or out themselves.

Two of the most common explanations for maintaining the status quo of separation is (1) giggling and (2) fear that kids won't be comfortable asking questions. These "problems" are routinely solved by teachers who acknowledge the nervous tension and calm everyone down, and by the use of an anonymous question box that permits students to ask about subjects too sensitive to air in public—like medical symptoms or physical or sexual abuse.

Perhaps the most important benefit of all-gender classrooms is that students learn a shared vocabulary, which disarms words that can be used to shock or to hurt. Mixed classes also give kids a way to practice communicating with one another across differences.

Tim Katz is a sexuality educator in Minneapolis who trains classroom teachers. "It's not enough to just do the biology," he says. "You have to address the fact that men don't have to think about menstruation or pregnancy prevention.

"Period empathy is something boys struggle with because they see that adult men are disengaged. Men act like menstruation isn't relevant to them, which reflects men's attitude toward women in general." For example, says Katz, "I might ask the boys in the room, 'How would you feel if that was happening to you?' or 'How could you support someone who is menstruating?'"

What wonderful questions, and happily there are many wonderful answers that deserve to be shared and celebrated.

Kamogelo Mampatla Betha, a thirty-one-year-old taxi driver in Limpopo, South Africa, ferries students to and from school. When he discovered toilet paper and bloodstains on the backseat, he realized that some of the girls couldn't afford pads, so he bought some and left them out on his dashboard, free to all. Some girls were too shy to take them, said Kamogelo, "And some of the boys make funny faces and remarks when they see that someone is menstruating. However, I have tried talking to them and explaining that this is normal." In South Africa, hit hard by the AIDS epidemic, free condoms are widely available. Kamogelo says, "If condoms can be made available, pads should, too."

When Hindo Kposowa founded the nonprofit Sierra Leone Rising (SLR) in 2006, the goal was to promote education, public health, and women's empowerment. Menstruation was not on the agenda, but when Kposowa learned that 24 percent of girls in his country were absent from school during their periods, he realized its impact on all of the organization's goals.

With assistance from the United Nations MHM program, SLR sends educators to rural schools to teach girls about the reproductive system, sex, sexually transmitted diseases, and menstruation. And working with The Pad Project, SLR created a program that employs local women to make washable cloth pads to distribute to students.

Kposowa decided to join the teaching teams as they visited schools. "It is my responsibility as a man, and for men across the world, to talk about menstruation. It isn't entirely up to women." He recalls being very nervous the first time he got up in front of a class. "I didn't know if girls would be comfortable for me to talk about this, but they were happy to see a man talking about period challenges, and also to offer solutions."

In fact, when Kposowa began handing out supplies, the girls rushed toward him. "I had to climb on a table!" he says.

The most famous male ally in the menstrual firmament is Arunachalam Muruganantham, an Indian inventor and social entrepreneur. The subject of two movies—the documentary *Menstrual Man* and the Bollywood comedy-drama blockbuster *Pad Man*—Muruganantham knew virtually nothing about menstruation until he got married. After learning that the vast majority of women in India could not afford disposable pads, he decided to create a low-cost alternative. The project became an obsession; the neighbors thought he was possessed by demons for asking women to test the prototype and, eventually, his wife left him.

After six years of trial and error, Muruganantham produced a small, easy-to-operate machine that rural women could use to make pads that they could also sell as a source of income and self-esteem. His invention won a local contest, which led to an appearance on television and offers from large companies that wanted to help him mass-produce his machine and "scale up." Muruganantham turned them down and even refused to copyright his invention, which inspired others in India and elsewhere to change, refine, and build models of their own.

Arunachalam Muruganantham's story also inspired Melissa Berton's class at Oakwood School to develop the project that became the subject of the documentary *Period. End of Sentence.*

Of course, not all men are freaked out by periods. Many are thoughtful, supportive, and wise. But as long as menstruation was unmentionable, there was no way of knowing who they were, or how they treated the menstruators in their lives.

The internet has become a source for their stories.

Several years ago, a Canadian woman posted a story about her father on Reddit.

"I was at school and bled through my skirt and chair. My dad had to come and pick me up.... I was crying, ashamed, didn't know what was happening. He felt bad, really badly. He took the day off, we got home, I washed, he washed my clothes, and then he took me to the store.

"We looked at pads together, he read them to me, we asked for the pharmacist's input and all. When we got home I had my own little 'period bag' that I'd bring around pretty much all my life until I got pregnant over a decade later. He also . . . kept a few pads in his car, in the glove compartment.

"Seventeen years later, I'm at my parents' house and my dad and I go for a drive. I wasn't expecting my period, but it happened . . . full blown. I started to look through my purse . . . to see if I had a pad. My dad sees me and asks if I'm looking for my phone or something. I tell him, 'No, just a pad.' He tells me, 'Oh, well just take a pad from the glove compartment. They're still there in case of emergency. Do you want me to pull over . . . ?'

"I almost had tears in my eyes. . . ."

Years later, that post still gets responses from grateful women and inspired dads, one of whom wrote, "As a father of 2 daughters (3 & 2) I am going to use your father as a role model. Tell him thanks for being awesome from a random internet stranger."

Another man wrote, "Wow, I need to learn from this. My daughter is 8. I never really thought about how to handle this other than to say, 'That's something to talk to your mom about.' But reading what you said makes me reconsider this. Thank you for posting this!"

Dads are also telling their own stories. Jon Vaughn, a single father from Australia, wrote about his older daughter's first period, which involved a visit to urgent care and a conversation about tampons versus pads. "This was the moment I'd been waiting for. Not the moment of getting her period . . . It was the moment that my fear was replaced with confidence in our ability to communicate as she gets older. . . . All those times I've told her, 'You can tell me anything,' was happening right now, live."

When big corporations feature good dads like these in ad

campaigns for period products, it's clear the struggle has gone mainstream. Procter & Gamble and Walmart hired actor James Van Der Beek to be the spokesdad for their #EndPeriodPoverty program. Van Der Beek, best known for his role on the TV series *Dawson's Creek*, and the father of four daughters, says, "I am a typical dumb guy; I did not know one in five girls deals with 'period poverty' in the US."

Hey Girls, a British company, hired stage and screen actor Sir Michael Sheen to speak for its #DadsforPads campaign. A scruffy every-dad, he stands in the period aisle of a supermarket and addresses his mates directly. "If you're out shopping with your daughter, you know what foods they like, right? But when it comes to pad and tampons you don't have a clue." After establishing his bona fides, Sheen says, "It can feel hard to start the conversation but that's okay," and signs off with, "Let's not leave dads out of the bloody conversation." Cheerio.

There are few models for young men who want to be friends and allies to the menstruators in their lives. One stellar example is *Absent*, a five-minute film produced by Freedom4Girls, a British nonprofit.

Absent: Synopsis

Chloe is waiting for the school bus when Josh, a fellow student, notices a period stain on the back of her pants. When they get inside, Josh sits beside her and mumbles, "You've got a mark."

She doesn't understand. "What?"

"A mark on your . . . ummm." When she realizes what he's saying, she stares out the window, completely mortified.

(Flashback to Chloe frantically trying to find a pad at home to no avail. Her mum apologizes; money is tight. Chloe improvises with a wad of toilet paper.)

Josh says, "I wasn't looking or anything, I just thought I'd tell you. My sister was like, umm, like the same." He hands Chloe his sweatshirt to cover up. "Here, use this," he says and changes seats, to save her from further embarrassment.

The Menstruation Business

A Short History of Period Products

Women have privately managed their menses for millennia with belts and pads made of fiber or repurposed cloth and other home-made paraphernalia. Multiple pregnancies were the norm for much of human history, which meant fewer periods over the course of a lifetime. But in the mid-nineteenth century, birthrates in the US and Europe declined dramatically, which led to an increase in menstruation. This alarmed some doctors, who claimed that pregnancy was the normal state of the female body and menstruation was a disease. But entrepreneurs saw an opportunity.

In 1867, a US patent was issued for a "vaginally inserted menstrual retentive cup," an elaborate mechanism that sent menses to an external pouch; thankfully, this thing never made it to market. However, by the 1890s, newspapers were running discreet advertisements for commercial belts, aprons, and gauze-covered cotton pads sold as "towels."

In 1920, Kimberly-Clark introduced Kotex, a disposable pad made of the same wood fiber found in World War I medical bandages—based on a menstrual workaround used by frontline nurses. Tampons went on sale in 1931, followed in 1937 by a rubber menstrual cup invented by the American actress Leona Chalmers. The idea of inserting a product into the vagina was a hard sell, especially after warnings that cups or tampons might impair virginity by breaking the hymen (not true), cause sexual arousal (absurd), or promote promiscuity (for crying out loud). In the 1970s, as more women joined the workforce and became more physically active, tampons gained in popularity, which slipped after a new super-absorbent tampon—the poorly named Rely—was linked to a dramatic spike in toxic shock syndrome (TSS), a serious and sometimes deadly infection. Cases of TSS fell dramatically after Rely was taken off the market, but tampon boxes still display warnings even though there is now only a one in 100,000 chance of contracting TSS from them. Pads have been the number one menstrual product in the US for a century, in part because of their familiarity. But consumers from the 1920s wouldn't recognize the current selection of menstrual pads: smaller, more absorbent, available in sizes to fit virtually everybody, and made with adhesive "wings" that put an end to the dreadful and dreaded menstrual belt.

Reusable cloth pads have been making a comeback—with "wings"—and the menstrual cup is finally having its moment. Leona Chalmers's 1937 latex menstrual cup went out of production during World War II due to a rubber shortage. She relaunched it during the early 1950s, calling it the Tassette (French for "little cup") and again in the late '60s with the disposable Tassaway, but both attempts failed. Today, cups are everywhere, produced by legacy companies like Procter & Gamble (founded 1837) and upstarts like OrganiCup (founded 2012); they are made of silicon, latex, or thermoplastic isomer, eco-friendly, efficient, and for those who can afford the up-front cost, an economical investment that can last for years.

There are also new products, such as absorbent underwear that minimizes the need for tampons or pads, and the single-use disposable menstrual ring.

The Business of Menstruation

The menstruation business is a multibillion-dollar industry with an expanding pool of products and players. It is a bonanza for global corporations, an opportunity for entrepreneurs—especially women—and a platform for education and empowerment. To make sense of the sprawl, I have sorted them into three categories: Big Period, New Period, and Social Enterprise Period.

Big Period includes large corporations and familiar brands, such as Johnson & Johnson, Procter & Gamble, Kimberly-Clark, Kao (China), Unicharm (Japan and Asia), and Essity (Sweden, with markets on four continents).

The survival of big consumer companies like these depends on transforming old products into "new and improved" ones, changing the packaging, or tweaking the design to keep regular customers engaged and to attract the next generation.

The youth market's interest in menstrual equity has driven Big Period to donate millions of dollars to local, national, and international nonprofits that distribute products and support menstrual health education. Of course, this largesse is not purely altruistic; there is solid evidence that "Business does well by doing good." International corporation Essity describes itself as "breaking barriers to well-being and contributing to a healthy, sustainable and circular society."

With enormous advertising budgets, Big Period is making a dent in menstrual stigma with period-positive advertising that reaches huge audiences, through public service campaigns (see "MENstruation," page 118), targeted commercials, and celebrity spokespeople:

The South African rapper, singer, actress, and poet Sho Madjozi starred in a commercial filmed in what she called "the loneliest aisle" in the supermarket where period products are sold and delivered a message about ending menstrual stigma.

In India, the Niine brand, having sponsored soccer clinics for boys and girls and posted banners at a men's cricket match, declares itself, "the first to create menstrual awareness, breaking the taboo."

In China, film star Zhou Dongyu faced the camera and spoke plainly. "It's unfortunate that menstruation has become a taboo topic, something that shouldn't be talked about publicly."

New Period companies have introduced innovations, reinvented many familiar products, and created new delivery and supply services. Few New Period products have achieved the name recognition of Thinx underwear or Diva menstrual cups, but this next-generation industry is fielding an international and diverse crop of entrepreneurs.

Many New Period companies share similar origin stories featuring young women who had a miserable period experience and/or see an unfilled need and decide to start a business. They do some market research, draw up a business plan, and launch a Kickstarter campaign to attract seed money from people who might use the product themselves or like to support eco-friendly and woman-owned businesses.

The organic-tampon company FLO was founded by two women who met as graduate students at the London School of Economics. Although organic products were available online, Tara Chandra and Susan Allen thought there was a mass market for them as well. In 2019, only two years after their Kickstarter campaign, their tampons were being stocked by BOOTS, a British pharmacy/health and beauty chain with twenty-five hundred stores. FLO donates products to organizations that fight period poverty in England and gives 5 percent of its profits to charities that support women and girls, including the Orchid Project, which works to end female genital mutilation.

Small companies have become proving grounds for innovation and inclusion, improvements and adaptive modifications. For example, Jane Hartman Adamé was having a hard time removing her menstrual cup—a fairly common problem for first-time users. The cups work by hugging the walls of the vaginal canal by means of a rubber ring at the top. To get it in and out, you have to be able to reach up and pinch the rim.

This is an awkward maneuver that requires wrist flexibility and hand strength, and because Adamé has Ehlers-Danlos syndrome, a connective-tissue disorder, that move could cause her to dislocate a wrist.

What Adamé needed was a more user-friendly cup. She enlisted a friend, Andy Miller, a medical device designer, and together they designed the Keela Cup, which has a loop at the bottom that attaches to the rim with a string; the string indents the ring and breaks the suction, so the cup is removed like a tampon.

A successful Kickstarter campaign followed, but production was a major challenge and in 2017, Lauren Schulte, founder of the Flex Company and creator of the Flex menstrual disk, acquired the rights to the Keela Cup design and brought the newly named Flex Cup to market. She also brought on Adamé and Miller as part of her team.

Adamé's story illustrates the benefits of inclusivity and diversity. As science and tech writer Rose Eveleth puts it, "Homogenous teams produce homogenous products for a very heterogeneous world. . . . The Keela Cup is just one example of what's possible when a diverse set of designers are involved in creating products."

Social Enterprise Period and New Period companies have a lot in common: young entrepreneurs, Kickstarter, and a commitment to helping women and girls. However, while the primary goal of a traditional business is to grow its bottom line, social enterprises are purpose driven. FLO's stated mission is "to create a product that is affordable, accessible and adorable." By contrast, Ruby Cup's mission is "To provide a sustainable and healthy menstrual hygiene solution for women and girls worldwide."

Ruby Cup was founded in 2011 in England by three young women who also met in business school. Maxie Matthiessen, Veronica D'Souza, and Julie Weigaard Kjaer believed that the menstrual cup was an affordable and sustainable alternative and wanted to make it accessible to those without a way or the means to get it. Ruby Cup's business model is "Buy One Give One," so for every menstrual cup sold online, another is given to charitable organizations in Nepal and throughout Africa; the company also sells the cups at a discount to nonprofits that distribute them for free.

Freweini Mebrahtu became world famous for her social enterprise company after being named CNN's 2019 Hero of the Year for her efforts "to educate girls about menstruation and remove the cultural stigma attached to periods."

Mebrahtu, an Ethiopian chemist, invented an inexpensive, reusable cloth pad to help girls who were missing school because they were menstruating. She first launched a company to make them in 2005, but it was a slow start. "It took me two years to get financing for the project because they didn't think anyone would buy it," she said. "I had to convince them that this is a basic necessity."

She persisted and was able to open the Mariam Seba Sanitary Products Factory, named after her daughter. In 2014, Mebrahtu entered into a partnership with Dignity Period, a nonprofit based in St. Louis, Missouri, which provides funds so pads can be distributed to schoolgirls free of charge. Her company, which produces 750,000 pads a year, is considered a model employer for providing its workers with training, four months of maternity leave, and free daycare.

Period-Adjacent Products

A lot of period-relevant merchandise did not exist ten years ago, and most of it doesn't get anywhere near bodily fluids. Big, New, and Social Enterprise companies are behind some of these products and services, but other kinds of businesses (like bakeries!) are also capitalizing on changes in the menstrual universe.

Education: Books that explain menstruation to girls used to be full of advice about staying fresh; recent titles are all about empowerment and body positivity, and there are a lot of them. An incomplete list for 2020 includes *My Menstrual Notebook*; *Your Moontime Magic*; *The Body Image Book for Girls*; and *Go with the Flow*, a graphic novel about middle school girls who buck the principal and organize to get pad machines installed in the school bathrooms.

Of course, today's "educational material" is not limited to the printed page. Among these: The Period Game, a board game created by students at the Rhode Island School of Design, for two to five players; Menstrupedia.com, a comic book from India that claims to be what "every girl must read as soon as she turns 9" and is available online in Hindi and ten other languages spoken in India, plus English, Bulgarian, Nepali, Russian, and Spanish; and Girlology.com, a subscription website full of information founded by two doctors who are also moms.

Period Party Gear: There may not be any greeting cards for a first period in your local drugstore yet, but they are available online, along with goods that testify to the growing popularity of period parties: invitations, napkins, uterus-shaped balloons, a "pin the ovaries on the uterus" game, and cookies shaped like pads and tampons. Gift options include a carrying case for period supplies, fuzzy heating pads for cramps, journals, scented candles, and chocolate in all shapes and sizes. Pure consumerism for sure, but there's no denying that the vibe and the merch is period positive.

Distribution: A company called Aunt Flo (no connection to FLO tampons) is betting that free pads and tampons will become the norm in public bathrooms. Its product list includes bathroom dispensers (no coins) that hold biodegradable pads and tampons (no plastic applicators) and eco-friendly waste systems.

The popularity of online shopping has spawned a number of subscription services—with pastel names like Blume, Kali, Lola, and Petal—that deliver monthly supplies of pads and/or tampons, some with a choice of "comfort" items: scented candles, bath oils, herbal tea, and, of course, chocolate.

Femtech: The term "Femtech" was coined in 2016 by Ida Tin, the founder of Clue, a period tracking app. Femtech employs software and technology to "support women's health," and has been involved in the development of absorbent period underwear and a wearable device for menstrual cramps that uses gel pads to deliver electric pulses at the site of pain. The sector is expected to be worth $50 billion by 2025.

Period.org

Business has jumped on the menstrual justice bandwagon, but the real work is being done in the nonprofit world, where activism takes place on many fronts and many levels: from high school drives, to organizing for policy changes in states and nations, to international campaigns for improved access to water, sanitation, and sexual-health education, and period supplies. The United Nations and academics in several disciplines are collecting and analyzing data about the impact of menstrual stigma and shame on women's lives. Environmental and health activists are raising alarms about menstrual waste and product safety.

There are scores of private nonprofit organizations working on a global scale, many of them began after a personal encounter with the needs of menstruators who had little or no access to period supplies. Celeste Mergens founded Days for Girls (DfG) in 2008 after she visited an orphanage in Nairobi, Kenya, where she learned that menstruating girls stayed in their dormitory rather than attend class because they lacked period supplies. "The image of them sitting on cardboard in their rooms kept me up that night, and that image never went away," she says.

When she returned to the United States, Mergens got to work and began collecting disposable pads to send to the students. She soon realized this was not a sustainable model and changed to cloth pads. Mergens recruited volunteers to sew the pads, a project that has grown to include teams and chapters in the US, Canada, the UK, Australia, and New Zealand. The kits they assemble (pads, shields, liners, underpants, washcloth, and soap) have reached more than a 1.7 million women and girls in more than a hundred countries.

Professor Chris Bobel, the author of three books about menstrual policy and politics, says she is "excited about global efforts to address menstruation," but as an "invested critic," as she identifies herself, Bobel challenges the emphasis on products shared by international agencies as well as private nonprofits. She questions the statistics and the message that the reason girls drop out of school in low-income countries is a lack of supplies, and points out other key factors in play, including the cost of school tuition and cultural and family pressures to marry early.

Bobel offers an important perspective about how the focus on menstrual "management" doesn't necessarily translate into challenging underlying causes, such as social stigma and the need for essential programs like comprehensive health education. The history of international philanthropy has tended to cast the relationship between people in low-income and high-income communities as victims and rescuers, with overtones of paternalism and racism. In this case, it can seem like the answer to menstrual injustice is delivering *products*.

The original mission statement of DfG was all about supplies: "To provide washable feminine hygiene kits to girls & women that would otherwise go without, enabling them to not miss valuable days from their education or employment."

Twelve years later, DfG volunteer groups still meet in church halls, sewing kits to send abroad. But the organization has changed and now supports social enterprise programs in countries where they are active. Local women run operations that make, sell, and distribute menstrual products, and who are also trained as women's health educators and advocates. DfG now describes its pupose as: "creating a more dignified, humane and sustainable world for girls through advocacy, reproductive health awareness, education and sustainable feminine hygiene."

"Products are an intersectional issue," says Mergens. "In the communities where we work, we talk about water, sanitation, and health, mortality, and childbirth. Products can be a bridge that allows us to talk about things that have been off the table, difficult things, like cutting [female genital mutilation], trafficking, abuse—basic human rights."

Melissa Berton, The Pad Project's founder, says, "Our aim is to raise awareness about how menstrual stigma and the lack of menstrual supplies inhibit women and girls from participating as equal citizens." The mission statement of The Pad Project actually says nothing about pads; its goal is "to cultivate local and global partnerships to end period stigma and to empower menstruators worldwide."

Mother Earth would like a word: Disposable period products are making a mess of the planet. In the United States, approximately 12 billion menstrual pads and 7 billion tampons are discarded every year.

In India, approximately 10 million tons of menstrual waste end up in landfills every year; the UK produces more than 200,000 tons.

Pads and tampons get flushed down toilets and clog sewers; many end up in the ocean, where they pose a threat to marine life or wash up onshore: period products are the fifth most common item found on Europe's beaches, more than straws or single-use coffee cups. Wherever they end up, there's a lot of plastic in the products, and plastic can take hundreds of years to decompose.

Solid waste is not even the most alarming environmental problem. Producing the plastics used in pads, tampon applicators, and packaging is an energy-intensive process that creates substantial fossil fuel emissions. In 2016, India classified menstrual products as "sanitary waste," which required incineration at "medical grade" temperatures of 800 degrees or higher. But because small incinerators in schools and other community settings don't get anywhere near that hot, period products are burned at lower temperatures that release potentially toxic gases into the atmosphere.

There is no simple or universal fix for the ecological impact of period product production and waste. Technical innovation and international regulatory agreements are key. Consumers can do their bit by buying tampons without plastic applicators or choosing biodegradable or cloth pads. Reusable period products are more effective at reducing waste and pollution, but they don't work for everyone: absorbent underwear is expensive; some cultures object to the use of menstrual cups on the grounds they break the hymen (they don't).

Environmentally minded consumers support eco-friendly New Period products and are the reason Big Period is redesigning goods and packaging. The English supermarket chain Sainsbury's stopped producing and selling its own brand of tampons with plastic applicators.

Health and Safety: Since 1995, the consumer group Women's Voices for the Earth has been raising alarms about the presence of toxins and allergens in products marketed to women. The organization led a successful campaign to rid a vaginal spray of harmful colorants, and in 2020 celebrated the passage of New York State's "Menstrual Right to Know Act," which requires tampon manufacturers to list all ingredients on product packaging.

Consumer complaints about chlorine dioxide in period products induced companies to stop using it, and "chlorine-free" appears on the labels of many Big Period and New Period products. There are continuing concerns about pesticides and toxins—specifically dioxin. The FDA requires tampons to be free of pesticide residue or show levels too low to pose a danger, but advocates counter that while the amount of dioxin in a single tampon is negligible, a lifetime of tampon use (by various estimates 12,000 to 14,000) may have adverse health effects.

Products sold as "organic" do not ensure the absence of dioxin. "Organic" or "natural" products are not necessarily safer. While those words are comforting, sometimes they are misleading. In 1995, the FDA ruled that menstrual sponges were "significant risk devices." Based on a comparison with commercial tampon users, sponge users had more bacteria in their vaginas—including *Staph aureus*, which causes toxic shock syndrome; another study found microscopic dirt and debris in sponges. And yet, menstrual sponges continue to be sold in stores and online as a natural alternative.

Some self-proclaimed homeopathic or traditional products are downright scary. Some companies sell "yoni pearls" that contain "traditional herbs" said to expel toxins, dead cells, bad bacteria, and old blood. These suppositories are supposed to stay in the vagina for a day or more. Other forms of snake oil include sitting over a pot of hot herbs to "tighten" the vagina and stuffing a jade egg up there to balance your hormones or connect to your feminine energy. Yikes.

There is virtually unanimous agreement among health professionals and consumer advocates that nobody should use scented products anywhere near and especially inside the vagina. Even self-proclaimed "natural" or "organic" sprays, wipes, and douches can cause itching, irritation, allergic reactions, and alter the pH balance of the vagina. They also perpetuate the incorrect and insidious belief that vaginas are dirty and smell bad.

Vaginas have a neutral odor. A foul smell means something is amiss and you should consult a health-care provider. "Your vagina is a self-cleaning oven," says Dr. Gunter. "It doesn't need your help. And there is no reason on earth a vagina should smell like a cucumber, or a rose, or a piña colada."

PART FIVE

Seeing Red

Red is the color of blood
Red is cool
Red tastes like a sour apple
Red smells like a rose
Red feels like mad
Reds sounds like a firecracker
Red makes me mad
Red is my favorite color

—Anonymous

I t isn't about anger, though righteous anger is certainly appropriate when the subject is menstrual stigma and shame.

Seeing red is making menstruation visible.

Seeing red means looking at the past through rose-colored glasses to find out how women managed their periods, how they talked about pain, whether they celebrated when a daughter came of age.

Seeing red is not gender-based, just as justice is not gender-based.

Seeing red means acknowledging nonbinary menstruators.

Seeing red means reading with new eyes and asking new questions.

Seeing red is cutting loose and making fun and making art.

It's getting harder to avoid seeing menstrual red. In the fall of 2020, Pantone, the global arbiter of color, announced a new shade called Period, which apparently has magical powers: "An active and adventurous red hue, courageous Period emboldens people who menstruate to feel proud of who they are. To own their period with self-assurance; to stand up and passionately celebrate the exciting and powerful life force they are born with; to urge everyone regardless of gender to feel comfortable to talk spontaneously and openly about this pure and natural bodily function."

Periods are breaking news and old news, a cause célèbre and a punch line. Periods show up in TV dramas and sitcoms, in plays and performance art, in film (documentary, animated, and feature) and poetry (spoken word and print). Menstrual blood is portrayed in photographs and paintings; human menses have even been used as a creative medium. Menstruation is so ubiquitous that, because you're reading this, you'll notice it everywhere, like the day you adopt a bulldog and suddenly see bulldogs on every street corner.

Advertising

The commercial begins with a Facebook post from "Richard" with an accusation of false advertising. Based on the commercials he's seen since childhood, Richard thought that a period was "the wonderful time of month . . . when the female gets to enjoy so many things; I mean bike riding, rollercoasters, dancing, parachuting." But when he "got a girlfriend" he was shocked to find out "there was no joy, no extreme sports."

The Cheshire-cat-cool announcer appears sympathetic. She admits that the ads do not represent reality and explains that the alternative universe Richard is upset about was the result of "research" showing that men can't handle the reality of menstruation, which she describes as "cramps and mood swings and the blood coursing from our uteri like a crimson landslide."

"You caught us," says the presenter, with a sly smile. "Well done, Richard."

Funny. Honest. Unapologetic. With a side of condescension. Welcome to the brave new world of period pride, which is on display in the arts—from oil painting, to installation art, to stand-up comedy, to marketing and advertising.

Especially advertising.

There is a long-standing debate about whether advertising mirrors or shapes social attitudes; in the case of menstrual products, the answer is . . . yes.

In the beginning, secrecy ruled, and you needed to know the code to understand what was being sold. A print ad from the 1870s featured a drawing of "a bandage suspender for the usual bandage." In the 1920s, the tagline for Modess was the single word "because," and one of its ads featured a "Silent Purchase Coupon" to present to the salesclerk for a completely wordless transaction.

In the 1940s and '50s, ads featured images of women wearing white dresses or pants, playing tennis, riding horses, or lying by the pool—unspoken testimony to how the sponsoring product would keep you safe from leakage. Athletic ads never went completely out of style, although the outfits got shorter and tighter, the sports got more extreme, and models now include Olympic athletes.

Early brands of tampons were given cute little names—Pursettes, Lil-Lets, and Fibs—that belied their bloody purpose. But the word "tampon" was not cleared for broadcast in the US until 1972. And it wasn't until 1985 that "period" was uttered in an American television ad.

Some US companies are leaning into the country's changing values about race and gender: refusing to pull ads that showed an interracial family at the breakfast table and ignoring homophobic complaints about two young men bringing home a couch. But too much honesty about menstruation appears to be a bridge too far.

American TV audiences are not going to see Bodyform's prize-winning 2017 "Blood Normal" commercial any time soon. Perhaps it was the image of a young couple in flagrante delicto, with a shot of menstrual blood trickling down the girl's leg. Or maybe it was the even more shocking use of bright red liquid poured onto a clean white pad—a colorful repudiation of the electric blue fluid that's been used to demonstrate absorbency for years.

Thinx, an American brand of absorbent period underwear, produced a commercial called "MENstruation" that portrayed a series of vignettes from a world where men have periods, too. You can watch it on online and decide for yourself which scene was the one considered too graphic for network broadcast. (I vote for the one showing a boys' locker room with a tampon string hanging out of someone's briefs.)

Creative marketers have put positive period messages to good use. In Germany, a public relations firm created a "Tampon Book," a forty-five-page illustrated volume about menstruation, with space inside to hide a box of tampons. Why? Because it was sold as a book, consumers were charged a 7 percent tax, rather than the 17 percent luxury rate then levied on period products, which has since been reduced.

When New York City graphic designer Erin Da Eun Song realized that homeless people needed period products, she created a poster with a cardboard pocket attached to encourage women who had tampons or pads to leave one for someone in need. She left posters and pads in bathrooms at New York's Penn Station, Union Square, Grand Central Terminal, and Port Authority Bus Terminal; when she returned a few hours later, her pads were gone and had been replaced by others, a godsend for the women who needed them, a reminder that period poverty exists, and a little victory for menstrual justice.

Comedy

Commercials and public relations campaigns about menstruation can be clever, but comedy takes it all the way to brazen.

In an episode of the TV series *Broad City*, co-creator and star Ilana Glazer smuggles her marijuana stash through airport security, confident that the period stain on her jeans would keep the TSA people at a distance. In a *Saturday Night Live* sketch, Phoebe Waller-Bridge appears in a commercial for "Tampax Secrets: Things you'd rather take out of your bag than a tampon." The things include a dead mouse, dog poop, a brick of cocaine, and a copy of *Mein Kampf*.

Australian comedian Mark Watson created a sublime two-and-a-half-minute film called "Men and Tampons in a Perfect World," in which two blokes talk about their respective wives' menstrual needs, problems, and products. They get worked up and foul-mouthed when the conversation turns to the value-added tax on period products, and the specter of toxic shock syndrome brings one of them to the point of outraged tears.

Stand-up comedy turns out to be the perfect platform for dissecting the lived experience and the stupid cruelties of periods.

Kate Clinton was among the first. "I would talk about menstrual amnesia, when you basically forget all about it. So, if your back hurts, you think, 'I must have lifted something heavy.' If you get cramps, you think, 'I must have eaten something that disagreed with me.'

"Blood on the couch? 'I must have cut myself shaving my legs.'"

Clinton says, "I was of the generation that still used menstrual pads and the belts that held them up, with that piece of shrapnel in front which inevitably got caught on your pubic hair. Then along came tampons, and if you sneezed it would blow your tampon out a quarter inch." She wanted to call her first album *Jokes from the Menstrual Tent*. That was 1981.

"People rolled their eyes. They had no idea what I was talking about." It's mainstream now, she says. "Erectile dysfunction opened the field."

Ali Wong, Amy Schumer, and many other comics tell personal period stories to hilarious effect, but nobody goes deeper into the red zone than Michelle Wolf. "I talk about periods a lot," she says in her stand-up special *Joke Show*. "I know they're gross. Periods are gross, but we gotta stop being cute."

Wolf is serious about getting rid of the word "cute," which the dictionary defines as "something pleasing in a nonthreatening way." She has nothing but scorn for euphemisms like "that time of the month." She suggests more vivid descriptions. "If you went into work and said, 'I've got bloody tissue falling out of a hole,' They'd be like, 'Take the week.'"

Says Wolf, "We have to stop being cute so we get the health care we deserve."

Even though it's no longer taboo, menstrual humor still has the power to startle, shock, and make trouble. It is not everyone's cup of tea, but it's not going to stop. At least, I hope not.

Menstrual Arts Hall of Fame

As menstruation emerges from the shadows, it is time to honor those who came before, turned on the lights, made trouble, taught, inspired, and celebrated the body that bleeds.

To that end, I propose a Menstrual Arts Hall of Fame, and nominate the following charter members:

Anonymous. The ancient Australian artist who depicted a pair of women holding sticks (or spears) above their heads. They seem to be in motion—dancing or hunting—as a stream of menstrual blood flows between their respective legs.

Anonymous. Indigenous Maori, date and tribal origin unknown, who wrote this poem/song/ritual incantation:

> The sun arising, coming forth
> Flying red, seeking its journey
> The moon arising, coming forth
> Flying red, seeking its journey
> One sees it dimly for the first time, dimly visible
> Are the company of supernatural beings
> Welcome, come forward
> The potential for life,
> The menstrual blood;
> Let life grow,
> Life itself, it lives.

Judy Blume (1938–). In her young adult novel *Are You There God? It's Me, Margaret.* published in 1970, Blume put period-talk on page one and didn't stop. Margaret is eagerly waiting for her first period, she worries that it will never come, bargains with God about it, and compares herself to other girls. There's not much information about menstruation in the book, but for millions of women it was a lifesaver, a rite of passage, and a source of comfort knowing they weren't abnormal for wondering, too. Dr. Jen Gunter, author of *The Vagina Bible*, says, "Thank God for Judy Blume."

Judy Chicago (1939–). The feminist artist is best known for the Dinner Party installation, a symbolic history of women that featured thirty-nine china plates painted with vivid, stylized images of vulvas. But eight years before the Dinner Party, Chicago exhibited a photolithograph of a woman—from the waist down—in the act of removing a tampon. It remains a surprising, honest, and beautiful image that makes you feel like a co-conspirator; still shocking in the best possible way.

Lucille Clifton (1936–2010). Winner of the National Book Award for Poetry, Clifton called menstruation a river: "beautiful and faithful and ancient" (see page ix). Someday the poem will be part of the junior high school English curriculum.

Emily Dickinson (1830–1886) did not write about menstruation explicitly; then again, "explicit" was not her style. And yet, her 1862 poem "The name—of it—is 'Autumn'—" is drenched in blood. Scholars have long assumed she was referring to the blood of Civil War battlefields, which is entirely possible. But read without the cultural blinders of menstrual shame, the Shower of Stain, and the upset basin suggest a more . . . personal interpretation.

Period. End of Sentence.

The name—of it—is "Autumn" —
The hue—of it—is Blood—
An Artery—upon the Hill—
A Vein—along the Road—

Great Globules—in the Alleys—
And Oh, the Shower of Stain—
When Winds—upset the Basin—
And spill the Scarlet Rain—

It sprinkles Bonnets—far below—
It gathers ruddy Pools—
Then—eddies like a Rose—away—
Upon Vermilion Wheels—

The Takeaway

Menstruation is not the curse, shame is the curse and shame threatens the health, well-being, and lives of millions. But shame, which has long seemed universal, hardwired, and inevitable, is starting to lose its grip because ...

- Students in college, high school, and middle school are winning the battle to put period products in their bathrooms, just like—and just as free as—toilet paper.

- Advocates and activists are pressing elected officials and policymakers to change unfair tax laws and provide free products in all public buildings.

- In 2018 the UN Commission on the Status of Women formally recognized menstruation as a matter of global development and recommended the promotion of "educational and health practices to foster a culture in which menstruation is recognized as healthy and natural and in which girls are not stigmatized on this basis."

- Menstruation is so newsworthy, it shows up in the business section, the "Living" section, international news roundups, and (when something really terrible happens) on the front page.

- Laughter is making stigma and misogyny look silly. As in the T-shirt that says "I'm on my period. What's your excuse?"

- Simple acts of kindness light the way forward, as when South African cabdriver Kamogelo Mampatla Betha put free pads on the dashboard of his taxi for schoolgirls and encouraged other cabbies to do the same. "It is important for all of us to help one another."

- Language is changing. "Menstruator" and "people who menstruate" have come into common use, acknowledging the fact that some nonbinary and trans people have periods. The New Zealand supermarket chain Countdown is getting rid of the signs that said "Feminine Hygiene" because, as per the press release, those words "give the impression that periods, which are an entirely natural part of life, are somehow something to hide to yourself, or that they're unhygienic." New signs will read "Sanitary Care" or "Period Products."

- Menstrual customs that put women in danger are being exposed and challenged. In 2005, Nepal outlawed *chhaupadi*—a practice that banished menstruating women and girls from their homes.

This is not to say the struggle is over, or that mistakes won't be made. Well-intentioned change can have unintended consequences: when outlawing *chhaupadi* did not stop women from sleeping in huts and hovels, the Nepali government tore down many of them, which drove some to seek shelter in even more dangerous places. It's going to take a long time before the world is safe and hospitable for everyone who menstruates. This is a revolution in the most human of human affairs, which means that change is bound to be uneven and halting.

While change on this scale defies prediction, it's helpful to set goals—to imagine a world where . . .

- Research about reproductive health is fully funded.

- Sexual-health education includes culturally diverse lessons about menstruation in relaxed, gender-inclusive classes.

- Checkups include taking a menstrual history and asking about changes or concerns, because menstruation is acknowledged to be a vital sign.

- Period products are affordable, untaxed, and subsidized, with reusable or compostable options, and manufactured with fair labor practices and minimal environmental impacts.

- All public bathrooms are stocked with free tampons and pads. All home bathrooms, too.

- Menstruation is not a roadblock to any form of employment.

- The term "feminine hygiene" is as archaic as "horse and buggy."

- Everybody knows the meaning of the word "menarche."

- Everybody knows how to pronounce the word menarche: *meh*-nark.

- A period stain on your pants might be embarrassing, but it's not a catastrophe.

- No one is shamed or bullied about menstruation.

Afterword

"If research hasn't changed you as a person,
you haven't done it right."

—Shawn Wilson, Cree scholar

For years, when readers of *The Red Tent* told me "I wish I had a red tent," I had a ready response.

"But you already have a red tent," I said. "It's called a book group. You meet monthly, eat and drink, share what's going on in your lives, and maybe you even get around to talking about the book." That always got a laugh.

I would also say, "I have no nostalgia for a time before antibiotics or anesthesia...or coffee." More laughter. "I know life is busy—maybe too busy. But I wouldn't want to give up any of the choices that go with my life today."

After a year of reading, thinking, talking, and writing about menstruation, my words sound defensive to me. I had heard the longing for a menstrual tent as a wish for a return to the past—or a gauzy version of a past where families lived together in harmony and women had easy access to their beloved sisters and friends, a Hallmark Channel fantasy of a "simpler time" that never really existed.

I have a very different reaction now. While I still hear a bit of misplaced nostalgia in the wish for a red tent, there is also an undertone of impatience with the secrecy that surrounds menstruation, a wish to replace "it's dirty" with "it's normal."

This represents a major change in how women think about their bodies, and change is risky. If women stop behaving as if we are perpetually cycle-free, we could lose hard-won advances and get sent back to the kitchen—a fear that explains resistance to the idea of menstrual leave.

After a large company in India announced the adoption of a period leave policy, journalist Barkha Dutt tweeted, "Period Leave . . . is exactly what ghettoizes women and strengthens biological determinism."

Dutt also said, "The other hideous thing about the idea of period leave is how it turns a normal biological experience into some sort of monumental event, gendering us at the workplace when we have fought so hard to not be gendered."

But she misses the bigger picture: her generic "workplace" is actually as "gendered" as a National Football League team in assuming that their workers don't bleed once a month.

Every public conversation about periods—whether it's menstrual leave, stigma, or access to period products—is really a conversation about power.

Gloria Steinem made that point in 1978 in a famous essay that imagined what it would be like if men—not women—menstruated. In that imaginary world, Congress would fund a National Institute of Dysmenorrhea to address work loss among men, while women would be pitied for a lack of innate math because they didn't have "the biological gift for measuring the cycle of the moon and planets." Also, women would not be welcome in the military or medical school because "they might faint at the sight of blood."

The mythical menstruating male has recently been reprised, but now he lives in a world where everyone has periods. In a vignette from a Thinx commercial called "MENstruation," a boy and girl in their underwear are seen kissing passionately. He stops and says, "I'm on my period." She smiles and says, "Me, too." They carry on.

In comedian Michelle Wolf's riff on a world where everybody menstruates, men have tampons with tiny superheroes on the end of the strings, but they're utterly clueless about menstrual hygiene. And women make fun of them.

Next-gen feminists (for lack of a better name) are not into a strictly binary view of the species: not all menstruators are women, not all women menstruate. Nor are they willing to hide any part of their identities: wise, silly, powerful, elegant, melancholy, fierce, sexual, or menstrual. They are ready to create a world in which a woman at a co-ed dinner party can stand up and ask, "Anyone have a tampon?"

The Red Tent: A Novel has inspired women in many countries to meet in teepees, crimson-decorated living rooms, bare church classrooms, and college dorms; also, in a women's prison in St. Petersburg, Florida, and at a conference dedicated to Black women's empowerment in Washington, D.C.

I'm pretty sure that menstruation is rarely front and center at these gatherings, but I know that they provide safe places for women and girls to relax and talk about everything and anything, including the hard stuff: abuse, sexual violence, harassment, fear, and grief. And I am deeply moved by the way my fictional tent has inspired so much creativity, community, and socially active sisterhood.

Whatever the red tent has come to stand for, it is not an avatar for nostalgia because the young leaders in the fight for menstrual justice aren't having any.

Talking about the politics of menstruation at the dinner table and in the public square—so recently unthinkable—seems to come naturally to them.

I look up to the kids who made the tampon cookies.

I am in awe of the teen who said she was NOT going to hide her pads in school.

I am inspired by the countless student activists who run community drives to collect pads and tampons for homeless women, and who agitate for period supplies in their school bathrooms because (duh) they're just as necessary as toilet paper and hand towels. And who take that experience out into the world, which they are changing.

Period. End of argument.

Acknowledgments

First, foremost, and forever, thanks to my husband, Jim Ball, for the saintly patience it takes to live with a writer on a deadline wrapped inside a quarantine. It was pretty much all menstruation all the time in my house, where Jim read multiple chapter drafts, cheered me on, and made wonderful meals week in and week out. What a guy.

Amy Hoffman and Stephen McCauley, my writing group partners, helped me find my way from despair to manuscript, as always.

I am grateful to the following people for expertise, consultation, research support, suggestions, and personal stories: Julie Abbate, Lisa Berman, Professor Chris Bobel, Carrie Bornstein, Charlie Ruth Castro, Dr. Charis Chambers, Kate Clinton, Lauren Corbett, Harry Diamant, Judy Elkin, Elaine Eva, Claudia Fox Tree, Bria Gadsden, Dr. Jen Gunter, Allegra Heath-Stout, Tim Katz, Nancy Kramer, Celeste Mergens, Dr. Joia Mukherjee, Ngāhuia Murphy, Judy Norsigian, Karen Rayne, Jane Redmont, Ketty Munaf Rosenfeld, Susannah Sirkin, Sondra Stein, Marcy Thomas, and Joanna Ware. I had the pleasure of learning from Irvienne Goldson, for thirty years a pioneering educator, health advocate, and mentor in Boston, whose untimely death in 2020 was a profound loss, but whose life continues to inspire.

Acknowledgments

Thanks to Emilia Diamant for research assistance and moral support, to Ande Zellman for her comments on early drafts and abiding faith in me, to Ineke Ceder and her eagle eye, and to Inga Logan McCarthy for the cheerleading and life-affirming baked goods.

I am indebted to a far-flung sounding board—people who listened, asked questions, and opined in ways that helped me get my arms around this multifaceted and burgeoning subject: Clary Binns, Tristan Binns, Ben Loeterman, Renee Loth, Barbara Penzner, Jonathan Strong, and Lorel Zar-Kessler.

Thanks to Roz Lippel and Rebekah Jett, my editors at Scribner, who made this a much better book, and to Amanda Urban, for making the match between me and The Pad Project.

I feel very fortunate to have connected with The Pad Project team and it was a pleasure working with Pad Project staff members Sorelle Cohen, Barret Helms, Mandakini Kakar, Rachel Wilson, and especially founder Melissa Berton, for her feedback, faith, and loving support.

I wrote this book while COVID-19 raged and ravaged, and as American politics devolved to new depths. I was fortunate to have spent a lot of that time within steps of the beautiful New England coastline, in the company of a small dog who didn't let me out of his sight.

The darkness of those days was brightened by learning about the passion, energy, and action of people around the world, demonstrating, demanding, and organizing for justice, equality, and the survival of the planet. Writing this book put me in virtual touch with people, some as young as twelve, who are fighting for menstrual justice, which is to say against sexism and patriarchy. They are using all means possible and making progress. They lift me up.

—Anita Diamant

Glossary

endometriosis: A condition where uterine tissue appears outside the uterus, which can cause cramps, heavy bleeding, and other symptoms.

feminine hygiene: A gendered and unfortunate term for menstrual products, given that "feminine" is commonly defined as "pretty" and "dainty," and "hygiene" implies the presence of dirt and disease.

feminism: Belief in the social, political, and economic equality of the sexes. The proposition that women are human beings.

fibroids: Common growths of the uterus that are noncancerous but can cause bleeding and pain.

menarche: A person's first period.

menopause: The permanent cessation of menstruation, a biological event that occurs only in humans, orcas, and short-finned pilot whales.

menses: The blood and tissue shed by the uterus during menstruation.

menstrual stigma: Disgrace, embarrassment, or humiliation associated with menstruation.

Glossary

menstruation: The regular shedding of the uterine lining, a word considered so embarrassing/shameful/inappropriate, there are some five thousand euphemisms for it, worldwide.

menstruator: A nongendered way to describe a person who menstruates.

misogyny: Prejudice against and distrust and dislike of women.

patriarchy: A social system in which men primarily hold power, based on a belief in male supremacy.

period poverty: Lack of access to menstrual products, to clean and safe toilets, to handwashing facilities and waste disposal, and to education about reproductive biology.

period shaming: Embarrassing, mocking, or humiliating people who menstruate.

stigma: A strong, culturally shared disapproval. Synonyms include disgrace, dishonor, slur, stain, taint. The opposite of "honor."

taboo: A subject too offensive for words; synonyms include distasteful, forbidden, unmentionable.

tampon tax: An umbrella term that includes all state and local sales tax and value-added and luxury taxes applied to pads, tampons, menstrual cups, etc., paid only by those people who need period products.

Notes

Introduction

4 *"The long silence"*: Janice Delaney, Mary Jane Lupton, and Emily Toth, *The Curse: A Cultural History of Menstruation* (Chicago, Urbana: University of Illinois Press, 1976), p. 174.

The Curse

9 *"Hansa, Northern Ethiopia"*: From a response to a Pad Project questionnaire, 2020.

9 *At any given moment, there are 800 million people menstruating*: www .undispatch.com/lets-talk-about-menstrual-hygiene.

9 *and as many as five thousand euphemisms*: From a 2016 survey of women in 190 countries, conducted by Clue, a period tracking app with the International Women's Health Coalition, https://helloclue.com/articles /culture/top-euphemisms-for-period-by-language.

10 *"When a woman has a discharge"*: *The Torah* (Philadelphia: Jewish Publication Society of America, 1962), p. 209.

11 *"Unto the woman He said"*: King James Bible, Genesis 3:16.

11 *The Catholic Church's rule against the ordination of women*: www.women priests.org/traditio/unclean.asp.

11 *For Hindus*: Aru Bhartiya, "Menstruation, Religion and Society," *International Journal of Social Science and Humanity* 3, no. 6 (November 2013): 523–27.

13 *Comedian Michelle Wolf*: *Nice Lady*, HBO, 2017.

Shame

16 *According to a 2018 survey of attitudes toward menstruation in New Zealand and Australia*: Brittany Keogh and Caroline Williams, "Period Shaming: Three in Four Kiwi Women say Menstruation Is Stigmatised," *Stuff*, August 2019, https://www.stuff.co.nz/life-style/115075228/period-shaming -three-in-four-kiwi-women-say-menstruation-is-stigmatised.

16 *Amanda in South Africa writes*: From a response to a Period Project questionnaire.

17 *In January 2019, Partabi Bogati died of smoke*: https://www.nytimes.com /2019/02/02/world/asia/nepal-menstruation-hut-death-chhaupadi.html.

17 *A month earlier, Amba Bohara*: https://www.nytimes.com/2019/01/09 /world/asia/nepal-menstruation-taboo.html.

17 *six months before that, it was Gauri Kumari Bayak*: https://www.nytimes .com/2018/06/19/world/asia/nepal-women-menstruation-period.html.

17 *In the small town of Sitatoli*: https://timesofindia.indiatimes.com/city /nagpur/where-women-are-banished-to-a-period-hut-with-no-power -or-loo/articleshow/66834713.cms.

18 *Comedian Michelle Wolf imagines*: *Michelle Wolf: Joke Show*, Netflix, 2019.

18 *Some parents assume that their children will learn*: State of the Period, poll commissioned by Thinx and PERIOD, conducted by Harris Poll, https:// cdn.shopify.com/s/files/1/0795/1599/files/State-of-the-Period-white -paper_Thinx_PERIOD.pdf.

18 *In a similar study from Quetta, Pakistan*: Judy Michael, Qaiser Iqbal, Sajjad Haider, et al., "Knowledge and practice of adolescent females about menstruation and menstruation hygiene visiting a public healthcare institute of Quetta, Pakistan," *BMC Women's Health*, January 2020.

19 *According to a 2019 UNICEF study, 50 percent of girls in Afghanistan*: Ruchi Kumar. "In Afghanistan, Replacing Shame with Understanding on the Topic of Menstruation," www.undark.org/2019/02/18/afghanistan-menstruation -taboo.

19 *Nearly the same results came out of a survey*: "Break the Barriers: Girls' Experiences of Menstruation in the UK," https://plan-uk.org/act-for -girls/girls-rights-in-the-uk/break-the-barriers-our-menstrual-mani festo.

20 *"Keep your menstrual status"*: Chris Bobel, *The Managed Body: Developing Girls and Menstrual Health in the Global South* (Switzerland: Palgrave Macmillan, 2019), p. 19.

20 *"medical gaslighting"*: "Thank God for Judy Blume," Dr. Jen Gunter, *New York Times*, November 21, 2019.

20 *her heavy flow had led to an iron deficiency*: Ibid.

20 *medicine viewed "female complaints"*: Ibid.

21 *associated with greater risk of dying before the age of seventy*: https://www .bmj.com/content/371/bmj.m3464.

23 *which is what happened when a Hindu priest in Gujarat*: https://www.hindu stantimes.com/india-news/menstruating-women-cooking-food-will-be -reborn-as-dogs-swami-narayan-sect-member/story-c9M4Ozcl0oilsYFE V4DfzN.html.

23 *reports surfaced about staff members at a college*: https://www.deccanher ald.com/national/sggi-college-that-stripped-60-girls-over-menstruation -shuts-website-four-arrested-805910.html.

23 *"India girl kills herself over 'menstruation shaming'"*: https://www.bbc.com /news/world-asia-india-41107982.

24 *Safreena lived in Southern India, in a relatively small city*: Reporting by Mandakini Kakar, documentary filmmaker and executive producer of the documentary *Period. End of Sentence.*

26 *Two years after Safreena died*: https://nation.africa/kenya/counties/bomet /bomet-girl-kills-self-after-humiliation-over-menses-202562.

Shamelessness: The Changing of the Guard

29 *"At 14, I hadn't yet learned the ropes of carrying pads"*: From Ashlie Juarbe, an illustrator and graphic designer in New York City, "My Period Made Me an Atheist," *The New School Free Press*, May 28, 2018. Used with the author's permission.

32 *Chelsea VonChaz*: Andrea Larson, "Meet Chelsea VonChaz," *The Fold*, October 16, 2019.

32 *Bria Gadsden is the co-founder*: www.loveyourmenses.com.

33 *In a 2019 survey, two thousand young American women*: Survey conducted by OnePoll in conjunction with Lunette Menstrual Cup, https://www.swns digital.com/2019/08/study-gen-z-more-open-to-talking-about-menstrua tion-than-millennials/.

33 *"My friend's 7th grader goes to a school"*: The message was posted by Ilyse Hogue, president of the National Abortion Rights League (NARAL). The location—state and city—of the tampon cookie caper was not made public, no doubt to protect the identities of the girls.

35 *Simone of Concord, North Carolina*: Email communication with The Pad Project.

36 *comedian Bert Kreischer*: "Bert Kreischer Threw His Daughter a Period Party," https://www.youtube.com/watch?v=bPN3Cc5i2RY.

Indigenous Wisdoms

41 *Scholar-activist Cutcha Risling Baldy calls*: Cutcha Risling Baldy, *We Are Dancing for You: Native Feminisms and the Revitalization of Women's Coming-of-Age Ceremonies* (Seattle: University of Washington Press, 2018), p. 77.

42 *being in sixth grade when the teacher called her*: Ibid., pp. 118–19.

43 *"That actual experience, living that experience in my body"*: Ibid., p. 134.

43 *"She does not know a time when men and women"*: Ibid., p. 146.

44 *"a tangible, physical, spiritual, and communal act of healing"*: Ibid., p. 128.

44 *"Long ago, before the world was bathed in light"*: Ngāhuia Murphy, *Waiwhero: He Whakahirahiratanga o te Ira Wahine* (*The Red Waters: A Celebration of Womanhood*) (Whakatane: He Puna Manawa Ltd., 2014), p. 7.

44 *"My wellspring of child-bearing"*: Ibid., p. 11.

45 *Murphy describes a culture*: Ibid., p. 17.

45 *In 1904, physician and amateur ethnographer*: Ngāhuia Murphy, *Te Awa Atua: (Menstruation in the Pre-Colonial Maori World)* (Whakatane: He Puna Manawa Ltd., 2013), pp. 93–94.

45 *Her goal is for girls "to create* tikanga *(a practice)"*: Ibid., p. 3.

46 *"If we reclaim menstruation"*: Ibid., p. 141.

46 *"It is a place women feel free to behave in ways they ordinarily don't"*: Wynne Maggi, *Our Women Are Free: Gender and Ethnicity in the Hindukush* (Ann Arbor: University of Michigan Press, 2001), p. 5.

47 *"Day after day"*: Colin M. Turnbull, *The Forest People* (New York: Touchstone, 1987), p. 187.

47 *A recording is available on YouTube*: https://www.youtube.com/watch?v =U7fuq910hWo.

New Traditions

49 *"Anyone can assert"*: Murphy, *Te Awa Atua*, p. 15.

51 *"[It] was a big day in our house"*: Published on the webpage of Dr. Christiane Northrup, author of *Women's Bodies, Women's Wisdom*, and other books about women's health and spirituality, www.drnorthrup.com/celebrating -a-girls-first-period.

51 *Women's groups of all affiliations*: Some New Moon, Red Tent, or Rosh Hodesh groups are affiliated with a religious institution, others are independent and freestanding; all provide support and a sense of community. A few examples of published ceremonies for menarche include http:// www.ritualwell.org/ (Jewish), www.unitariancongregation.org, and www .WitchesandPagans.com.

51 *Rabbi Elyse Goldstein writes*: *Lilith* magazine, Spring 1991.

53 *A meditation for menarche*: Created by Matia Rania Angelou, Deborah Issokson, and Judith D. Kummer, for Mayyim Hayyim Living Waters Community Mikveh and Education Center, Newton, Massachusetts. Used with permission. www.mayyimhayyim.org.

53 *A meditation for menopause:* From "Upon Reaching Menopause: An immersion ceremony," ibid.

Period Poverty and the Tampon Tax

59 *menstruators spend $17,000 during their lifetime*: https://dollarsandsense
.sg/ladies-heres-much-period-costs-lifetime/.

60 *In 2020, Alabama, Arkansas*: https://taxfoundation.org/2020-sales-taxes/.

62 *As Weiss-Wolf writes in her book*: Jennifer Weiss-Wolf, *Periods Gone Public: Taking a Stand for Menstrual Equity* (New York: Arcade Publishing, 2017).

62 *Scotland is the world leader*: https://www.theguardian.com/society/2018
/feb/05/period-poverty-scotland-poll-shows-women-go-to-desperate
-lengths.

62 *And in 2020, the Scottish parliament*: https://www.theguardian.com/uk
-news/2020/nov/24/Scotland-becomes-first-nation-to-provide-free-period
-products-for-all.

Menstruating at Work

63 *Just under half*: http://www.catalyst.org/research/women-in-the-workforce
-global. Diva Dhar, "Women's unpaid care work has been unmeasured and undervalued for too long," King's College London, News Centre, January 14, 2020, https://www.kcl.ac.uk/news/womens-unpaid-care-work-has-been
-unmeasured-and-undervalued-for-too-long.

63 *A 2019 US Bureau of Labor Statistics report*: https://www.bls.gov/news
.release/famee.nr0.htm.

64 *When the epidemic reached crisis proportions*: https://www.scmp.com/com
ment/opinion/article/3052524/how-chinas-coronavirus-health-care
-workers-exposed-taboo.

65 *Women comprise 90 percent of the nearly 40 million*: Anna Dahlqvist, *It's Only Blood: Shattering the Taboo of Menstruation* (London: Zed Books, 2018), p. 108.

65 *Seventy percent of those who responded*: Ibid., p. 114.

65 *"There is no research into how menstruators"*: Ibid., p. 120.

65 *Manufacturers in Dhaka began to provide subsidized period products*: Ibid., pp. 118–19.

66 *According to the United Nations International Labor Organization*: www.ilo
.org/safework/areasofwork/hazardous-work.

66 *the seventh woman in her family to have her uterus removed*: https://
www.thehindu.com/news/national/other-states/in-beed-a-harvest-of
-crushed-hopes/article28969404.ece. "Why many women in Maharatra's
Beed district have no wombs," www.thehindubusinessline.com/economy
/agri-business/why-half-the-women-in-maharashtras-beed-district-have
-no-wombs/article26773974.ece.

66 *Contractors hire couples as a single unit*: https://www.thehindu.com/news
/national/other-states/in-beed-a-harvest-of-crushed-hopes/article2896
9404.ece.

67 *There is also data that implicates*: Ibid.

67 *the number of procedures*: Ibid.

69 *help lifting heavy objects*: https://www.bbc.com/news/world-asia-5059
7405.

69 *However, up to 20 percent of women*: American Academy of Family Physicians, https://www.aafp.org/afp/2012/0215/p386.html.

70 *Jeanette MacDonald, a Hollywood star*: Gary Carey, *Anita Loos: A Biography*
(New York: Knopf, 1988), pp. 164–65.

71 *an online petition proposing national laws*: www.change.org/p/the-indian
-government-make-laws-policy-declaring-menstrual-leave-for-women.

71 *Journalist Barkha Dutt reprised a fiery opinion piece*: www.washingtonpost
.com/news/global-opinions/wp/2017/08/03/im-a-feminist-but-giving
-women-a-day-off-for-their-period-is-a-stupid-idea.

71 *Zomato, one of India's largest food-delivery firms*: Geneva Abdul, "Company's
Paid Leave Plan Takes on a Workplace Taboo," *New York Times*, August 11,
2020, www.nytimes.com/2020/08/11/business/india-zomato-period-leave
.html.

71 *"It's almost as if the over-40s"*: Caitlin Fitzsimmons, "Menstrual Leave the
New 'Woke' Workplace Right," *Sydney Morning Herald*, August 18, 2019.

72 *"It challenges the notion of the 'ideal worker'"*: Ibid.

Dignity

73 *In 2016 . . . the American Academy of Pediatrics and the American College of Obstetricians and Gynecologists issued policies*: https://pediatrics.aap publications.org/content/138/1/e20160295.

74 *from "I hate it"*: https://rewirenewsgroup.com/article/2016/08/04/center ing-disabled-people-conversations-menstruation/.

74 *"The older black women in my life"*: https://www.shethinx.com/blogs/thinx -piece/free-bleeding-embrace-my-flow.

74 *less likely to receive pain medication*: "Defining Racial and Ethnic Disparities in Pain Management," www.ncbi.nlm.nih.gov/pmc/articles/PMC3111792/.

74 *In a 2016 survey of 222 medical students and residents*: www.pnas.org/con tent/113/16/4296.

75 *The American Medical Association acknowledged the problem in 2002*: Brian D. Smedley, Adrienne Y. Stith, Alan R. Nelson, eds., *Unequal Treatment: Confronting Racial and Ethnic Disparities in Health Care* (Washington, DC: National Academies Press, 2003), p. 440.

75 *Black patients receive better care*: https://labblog.uofmhealth.org/rounds /minority-patients-benefit-from-having-minority-doctors-but-thats-a -hard-match-to-make-0.

75 *"Black women will come and say, 'Oh great'"*: www.bet.com/news/national /2019/11/04/op-ed—more-people-are-talking-about-black-womens-pe riods-and-th.html.

75 *the chances are slim*: www.pubmed.ncbi.nlm.nih.gov/26646119.

76 *The Period Doctor*: www.theperioddoctor.com.

76 *The medical community has documented*: https://www.nature.com/articles /d41586-019-03228-6.

76 *"The medical community largely avoids talking"*: https://www.wbur.org/cog noscenti/2020/06/12/anti-racism-in-medicine-hospitals-ayotomiwa-ojo.

77 *The United States has only 5 percent*: https://www.prisonpolicy.org/global /women/2018.html.

77 *More than 200,000 women are incarcerated*: https://www.sentencingpro ject.org/issues/racial-disparity/. Black women are twice as likely as white women to be incarcerated, Latinx women are 1.3 times as likely; Native American women are four times as likely to be imprisoned.

77 *that rule applied*: https://worldpopulationreview.com/countries/united-states-population. (Within the juvenile justice system, the racial disparities follow the same pattern, and 40 percent of those incarcerated as juveniles identify as lesbian, bi-sexual, or transsexual.)

78 *In 2014, a group of prisoners in Michigan filed a lawsuit*: https://www.mlive.com/news/muskegon/2014/12/michigan_aclu_files_lawsuit_ag.html.

78 *In Connecticut, two women sharing a cell*: https://www.theguardian.com/commentisfree/2015/jun/12/prisons-menstrual-pads-humiliate-women-violate-rights.

78 *A 2015 report about conditions in New York State's women's prisons*: https://static.prisonpolicy.org/scans/Reproductive-Injustice-FULL-REPORT-FINAL-2-11-15.pdf.

78 *Chandra Bozelko, a blogger, author, and activist*: https://www.urbo.com/content/depressing-facts-about-being-a-woman-in-prison-you-didnt-know.

78 *Kimberly Haven, another formerly incarcerated prison activist*: https://www.aclu.org/news/prisoners-rights/why-im-fighting-for-menstrual-equity-in-prison.

78 *Tutwiler was called "a toxic environment"*: https://www.justice.gov/opa/pr/justice-department-releases-findings-showing-alabama-department-corrections-fails-protect.

79 *In her testimony before the legislature, Adrienne Kitcheyan*: https://www.phoenixnewtimes.com/news/male-lawmakers-vote-female-inmates-have-unlimited-tampons-10108929.

81 *By 2019, 235,000 Canadians experienced homelessness*: www.thecanadianencyclopedia.ca/en/article/homelessness-in-canada.

81 *domestic violence has been cited as a leading cause*: www.invisiblepeople.tv/domestic-violence-in-canada-causing-rise-in-family-homelessness.

82 *from "Home," a poem by Warsan Shire*: https://www.facinghistory.org/standing-up-hatred-intolerance/warson-shire-home.

82 *According to the United Nations Refugee Agency (UNHCR), 37,000 people*: https://www.unhcr.org/globaltrends2018/.

82 *UNHCR estimates that there were more than 70 million*: Ibid.

83 *This perfect storm of indignities violates the 2018 United Nations*: https://menstrualhygieneday.org/significant-new-language-mhm-human-rights-council-resolution-ahrc39l-11/.

83 *In the summer of 2019, conditions in detention centers on the US–Mexico border*: https://www.independent.co.uk/news/world/americas/trump-immigration-migrant-children-border-lawsuit-period-tampon-latest-a9081341.html.

84 *Marni Sommer, professor at the Columbia University Mailman School of Public Health*: https://www.ncbi.nlm.nih.gov/pmc/articles/PMC3780686/.

Men-struation

89 *post the dumbest thing a man had ever said to them about periods*: Karolina Wv, https://www.boredpanda.com/dumbest-thing-man-said-to-women-reproductive-health-menstruation.

90 *YKA (Voice of Youth), a youth social media platform*: A media platform, founded in 2008, that invites readers to weigh in on social justice issues, https://www.youthkiawaaz.com/periodpaath/.

92 *Kamogelo Mampatla Betha, a thirty-one-year-old*: https://www.goodthingsguy.com/people/taxi-driver-keeps-sanitary-pads-in-car-for-underprivileged-girls/.

93 *Hindo Kposowa founded the nonprofit Sierra Leone Rising*: https://www.sierraleonerising.org.

94 *and even refused to copyright his invention*: Muruganantham's example inspired others to produce low-cost machines around the world. In 2014, Amy Peake, an inventor and the founder of Loving Humanity, placed the first pad machine in the Jordanian Zaatari refugee camp, which housed 79,000 people at the time, www.lovinghumanity.org.uk. In India, Suhani Mohan quit her job as an investment banker to start Saral Designs (www.saraldesigns.in), which manufactures semi- and fully automated pad machines.

94 *"I was at school and bled through"*: "Grateful for my dad who year after year isn't grossed out by 'women's stuff,'" www.reddit.com/r/TwoXChromosomes/comments/4w4m53.

95 *"As a father of 2 daughters (3 & 2)"*: Almie Rose, "What This Dad Did for His Daughter Sets a Standard," August 4, 2016, https://archive.attn.com/stories/10468/index.html.

95 *"This was the moment I'd been waiting for"*: https://goodmenproject.com/families/confidence-that-bleeds.

96   Absent, *a five-minute film*: https://www.youtube.com/watch?v=C2zd1x4
     e4ds. Also worth watching: *Her First Time*, a prize-winning eight-minute
     film from India, in which the father plays a small but important support-
     ing role in a story told from the mother's perspective about their daugh-
     ter's menarche, www.youtube.com/watch?v=_XvTV7R2FN8.

The Menstruation Business

101 *"Business does well by doing good"*: https://www.sciencedirect.com/science
     /article/pii/S0007681306001674.

103 *Jane Hartman Adamé was having a hard time*: https://www.vice.com
     /en_us/article/vbk5ky/keela-flex-menstrual-cup-design-bias.

104 *As science and tech writer Rose Eveleth*: Ibid.

106 *the growing popularity of period parties*: Allison Sadlier, "More mothers
     are planning to throw their daughters a 'period party,'" *New York Post*,
     March 4, 2020.

106 *The term "Femtech" was coined*: www.femtechinsider.com.

106 *The sector is expected*: https://www.statista.com/statistics/1125599/fem
     tech-market-size-worldwide/.

Period.org

107 *.org*: Most nonprofit organizations use the .org domain. However, the des-
     ignation is not vetted or regulated and can be purchased by anyone. Only
     legally recognized nonprofits can use .ngo and .ong domains.

108 *The kits they assemble*: www.daysforgirls.org.

109 *In the United States, approximately 12 billion menstrual*: https://stanford
     mag.org/contents/planet-friendly-periods.

110 *In India, approximately 10 million tons*: https://swachhindia.ndtv.com
     /urgent-challenge-india-needs-tackle-menstrual-waste-6665/.

110 *the UK produces more than 200,000 tons*: https://www.london.gov.uk/sites
     /default/files/plastics_unflushables_-_submited_evidence.pdf.

110 *plastic can take hundreds of years to decompose*: https://www.citytosea .org.uk/campaign/plastic-free-periods/.

110 *lower temperatures that release potentially toxic gases into the atmosphere*: https://jodoindia.org/the-real-meaning-of-menstrual-pollution/.

110 *The English supermarket chain Sainsbury's*: https://theecologist.org/2019 /aug/21/sainsburys-ditches-plastic-tampon-applicators.

111 *by various estimates 12,000 to 14,000*: https://www.thedailybeast.com /save-the-planet-ditch-the-tampon.

111 *In 1995, the FDA ruled that menstrual sponges*: https://www.fda.gov/regu latory-information/search-fda-guidance-documents/cpg-sec-345300 -menstrual-sponges.

112 *"Your vagina is a self-cleaning oven"*: https://www.rnz.co.nz/national/pro grammes/afternoons/audio/2018690238/dr-jen-gunter-why-we-need-to -challenge-pseudoscience.

Seeing Red

118 *Bodyform's prize-winning 2017 "Blood Normal" commercial*: "Blood Normal" won first prize at the 2018 Cannes Lion International Festival of Creativity, a global event for the creative communications, advertising, and related fields. Bodyform is part of Essity, a global company based in Sweden, https://www.youtube.com/watch?v=xr57Tl1Yw2s.

118 *In Germany, a public relations firm created a "Tampon Book"*: https://www .mhpbooks.com/packaging-tampons-as-books-the-subversive-new-way -to-avoid-a-sexist-tax/.

119 *Australian comedian Mark Watson created a sublime two-and-a-half-minute film*: https://www.youtube.com/watch?v=Z5pNv-WXRc8.

121 *The ancient Australian artist*: Pilbara Region NW Australia, petroglyphs in the region may be among the world's oldest examples of rock art, https:// www.australiangeographic.com.au/news/2013/04/burrup-peninsula -rock-art-among-worlds-oldest/.

121 *Indigenous Maori, date and tribal origin unknown*: Translation by George Grey, British colonial governor of New Zealand, 1853. Murphy, *Waiwhero*, p. 10.

122 *"Thank God for Judy Blume"*: https://www.nytimes.com/2019/11/21/style /menstrual-diarrhea-happens.html.

Afterword

130 *"The other hideous thing about the idea of period leave"*: https://www.alja zeera.com/news/2020/8/12/zomatos-period-leave-policy-triggers -debate-among-indian-women.

130 *Gloria Steinem made that point in 1978 in a famous essay*: Ms., October 1978.

Index

Index

Chery, Magdala, 75
chhaupadi, 16, 126
Chicago, Judy, 122
Ch'ilwa:l (Flower Dance), 42–44, 48
China, 64, 102
chlorine dioxide, 111
Christianity, 11
Clifton, Lucille, ix, 122
Clinton, Kate, 120
Clue, 106, 137n
CNN, 104
comedy, 119–20, 126
confirmation, 50
Congo Basin, 47
Constitution, US, 78
Countdown, 126
COVID-19 (coronavirus) pandemic, 5,
    61, 64
Cullors, Patrisse, 36
"curse, the," 5, 9–13, 39, 49, 125
Curse, The (Delaney, Lupton, and
    Toth), 4
customs, *see* traditions

Dahlqvist, Anna, 65
Daimaru, 69
Days for Girls (DfG), 107–9
Delaney, Janice, 4
Department of Justice (DOJ), 78, 80
Dickinson, Emily, 122–23
dignity, *see* menstrual dignity
Dignity Period, 105
Dinner Party, 122
dioxin, 111
disabilities, 73–74
doctors, 20, 21, 67, 75–76
    see also health care
D'Souza, Veronica, 104
Dutt, Barkha, 71, 130
dysmenorrhea, 69–70

education
    health, 108
    about menstruation, 105–6,
        125

about menstruation, lack of, xiv, 2,
    3, 15, 17–21, 34, 91
    sexual-health, 91–92
    see also school
elima, 47, 48
endometriosis, 20, 74, 135
environment, 111–12
Essity, 101, 148n
euphemisms for menstruation, 9,
    120
Eve, 11
Eveleth, Rose, 104

factory workers, 67–68
fathers, 90, 94–96
FDA (Food and Drug
    Administration), 111
federal assistance programs, 61
Federal Bureau of Prisons, 77, 79
feminine hygiene, use of term, 22, 126,
    135
Feminine Mystique, The (Friedan), 63
feminism, feminists, 73, 131, 135
Feminist Majority Foundation,
    xv–xvi
Femtech, 106
fibroids, 20, 74, 135
Flex Cup, 103–4
FLO, 102–4
Flower Dance, 42–44, 48
Forest People, The (Turnbull), 47
Freedom4Girls, 96
Free the Tampons Foundation, 62
Friedan, Betty, 63

Gable, Clark, 70
Gadsden, Bria, 32, 76
Gandhi, Indira, 68
Gandhi, Mohandas, 12
garment workers, 67
Garza, Alicia, 36
gender, xix, 115, 118
Gen Z women, 32, 36
Girdauskas, Jana, 81
girls, use of word, xix

Index

menstrual stigma, xiv–xv, xvii, xix, 5, 13, 17, 21–23, 30, 33–34, 81–83, 104, 107–9, 125, 126, 135
  advertising and, 101–2
  in Black community, 74, 76
  see also menstrual dignity
menstruation, 136
  as "the curse," 5, 9–13, 39, 49, 125
  dysmenorrhea and, 69–70
  education about, 105–6, 125
  euphemisms for, 9, 120
  heavy, 20, 21
  irregular, 21
  lack of knowledge or misinformation about, xiv, 2, 3, 15, 17–21, 34, 91
  making visible, 115–23
  "normal," 20–21
  pain during, 20, 21, 69–70
  sequestration during, 16–17, 46–47, 126
  silence about, 2, 3, 4–5, 17–19, 29–31, 34, 65, 87
  as threat, 10–11
menstruator, use of word, xix, 126, 136
Mergens, Celeste, 107–9
#MeToo movement, 5
mikveh, 11
Millennials, 31–33, 36
Miller, Andy, 103
Mink, Patsy, 68
misogyny, xix, 5, 92, 126
Modess, 117
Mohan, Suhani, 146n
moko kauae, 45
Movement for Black Lives, 36
Muhammad, Prophet, 12
"Munich Mannequins, The" (Plath), xviii
Murphy, Ngāhuia, 44–46, 49, 52
Muruganantham, Arunachalam, xiv, xvi, 3, 93–94, 146n
"My Period Made Me an Atheist" (Juarbe), 29–31

Nachmanides, 11
NASA, 89
National Alliance to End Homelessness, 80
Native Americans, 43–44, 80
  Hoopa Valley Tribe, 42, 43
Nepal, 16–17, 126–27
New Moon groups, 141n
New York, 62, 111
New Zealand, 16, 44
Niine, 102
Nobel Peace Prize, 36
nonbinary people, xix, 4, 22, 77, 80, 91, 115, 126, 131
nonprofit organizations, 101, 107–8, 147n
Northrup, Christiane, 141n
Nyong'o, Lupita, 15

Oakwood School, xv, xvi, 4, 94
Ojo, Ayotomiwa, 76–77
Once-a-Month, 33
Orchid Project, 103
OrganiCup, 100
Our Women Are Free (Maggi), 46

Pacific Island women, 80
Pad Man, 93
Pad Project, The, xiv–xvii, 2, 35, 93, 109
Pakistan, 46
Pantone, 116
Papatuanuku, 44, 45
Passaris, Esther, 26
patriarchy, xiv, 30, 134
Peake, Amy, 146n
Period. End of Sentence. (film), xiv–xvii, 2–4, 15, 34, 94
period, use of word, 9, 117
Period Equity, 61
Period Feast, 23
period parties, 35–36, 106
"Period Path" contest, 90
period poverty, xiii–xiv, 4, 5, 35, 57, 59–63, 81, 96, 136

Index

About the Author

Anita Diamant is the author of five novels, including *The Boston Girl* and *The Red Tent*; the collection of essays *Pitching My Tent*; and six nonfiction guides to contemporary Jewish life. Her articles and essays have appeared in *the Boston Globe*, the *Wall Street Journal*, and *Parenting*, among other publications.

Visit her website at AnitaDiamant.com.

PERIOD.
END OF SENTENCE.

Best-selling author and award-winning journalist Anita Diamant explores the subject of menstruation, from toxic historic and religious roots to how young activists are challenging the silence and shame that can erode self-esteem and even threaten lives; from Indigenous traditions that honor and celebrate this essential element of human life to the ways that popular culture is dismantling period stigma, one pad at a time, one joke at a time.

Inspired by The Pad Project's Oscar-winning film, *Period. End of Sentence*, Diamant examines the quickly evolving international movement for change in a timely and engaging investigation that will transform the way we think about periods.

Discussion Questions

1. Share a memory of your first period and/or of how you first learned about menstruation.

2. Are you comfortable talking about periods with friends and/or family? Have you ever discussed menstruation with someone of a different gender than your own? Do you think conversations about menstruation are easier now that the topic is less taboo in popular culture and the media?

3. Diamant writes: "Basic menstrual literacy is essential and potentially lifesaving. Everyone needs to know that a 'normal' period is different for everybody. . . ." Are you comfortable asking your health care provider about your periods? Has a health care provider ever asked you about your menstrual health or history?

4. The chapter "New Traditions" (page 49) describes how some cultures and families celebrate menarche in ways ranging from traditional to innovative. If you could invent a meaningful way

to acknowledge a first period for yourself or someone you know, what would it look like?

5. Discuss the term "period poverty" (page 59). Have you or someone you know experienced period poverty? How might you address period poverty in your community?

6. In Scotland, the Period Products Act of 2020 mandated that period products be provided for free to anyone in the nation who needs them. Does your school or place of business provide free menstrual supplies? If so, when and how did that policy come about?

7. Consider the arguments (pages 63–72) in favor of and against menstrual leave in the workplace. In your opinion, does menstrual leave advance or threaten women's progress and status?

8. Discuss the contrast between the way menstruating women are sequestered among the Kalasha people in northern Pakistan (page 46)—somewhat reminiscent of practices described in Diamant's novel *The Red Tent*—versus the danger posed by menstrual separation in parts of rural Nepal (page 104).

9. Google "menstruation in the news" and select a story that interests/surprises/resonates with you. What did you learn that you didn't know? What questions does it raise?

10. In "The Menstruation Business," Diamant discusses recent trends in menstrual products, including new products such as menstrual cups, period underwear, cloth pads, period apps,

etc. Have you or anyone you know tried any of these? Do you think you might in the future?

11. After reading *Period. End of Sentence,* do you agree with the statement, "period supplies . . . are just as necessary as toilet paper and hand towels"? What would it mean to you and/or to the general public if pads and tampons were free in all public bathrooms?

12. What would you add to Diamant's list of goals in "The Take-away?"